TREES OF NOVA SCOTIA

TREES
OF NOVA SCOTIA
A Guide to the Native and Exotic Species

GARY L. SAUNDERS

Illustrations by
ELIZABETH OWEN

Nimbus Publishing
and the
Nova Scotia Department of Natural Resources

Co-published by the Province of Nova Scotia and Nimbus Publishing Limited
Sponsoring department: Department of Natural Resources
A product of the Nova Scotia Government Co-publishing Program

Design: Kathy Kaulbach, Halifax
Cover film: NS Digital Technologies Inc., Halifax
Printing & binding: McCurdy Printing (1995) Limited, Halifax

Originally produced under the Canada-Nova Scotia Forest Resource Development Agreement.

To ensure that the information contained in this book continues to accurately reflect the significance of Nova Scotia's trees, the text was revised in 1995 by Emily Gratton of the Nova Scotia Department of Natural Resources' Education and Publication Services Division. Technical advice was provided by Tim Whynot, a forester with DNR's Extension Services Division.

Canadian Cataloguing in Publication Data
Saunders, Gary L.
Trees of Nova Scotia
[3rd] rev. ed.
ISBN 1-55109-123-2
Co-published by the Province of Nova Scotia.
Includes bibliographical references and index.
1. Trees—Nova Scotia—Identification. I. Owen, Elizabeth.
II. Nova Scotia Museum. III. Title.
QK203.N6S28 1996   582.1609716   C95-950314-5

MAP OF NOVA SCOTIA

CONTENTS

PREFACE

To a stranger, a big city can seem the loneliest place on earth. Until you get to know your way around, the faces are just faces and the buildings are just buildings. It is the same with the world of nature. A field or a forest may teem with life. Yet until you really get to know these landscapes and their inhabitants, the field may be just a lot of grass and the forest just a lot of trees. It is our loss if we treat them as such.

We in Nova Scotia are notably rich in materials for nature study. Above all, we are rich in trees. Forests cover almost 75 per cent of Nova Scotia's land area. Moreover, our ancestors had the foresight to plant many trees about our towns and farmsteads. Thanks to our mild climate, more kinds of trees thrive here than one might expect for these latitudes.

All this being so, we stand to gain much by learning more about trees. After all, why should only those who work around trees be able to tell a white pine from a red pine, or a paper birch from a yellow birch? Such things should be part of the lore of our people and should be passed from one generation to another.

This is important, because bound up with a knowledge of trees is a knowledge of animals, of birds, of plants, and of insects. In a province such as ours, trees are often at the base of the life pyramid, as well as the economic pyramid.

ACKNOWLEDGEMENTS

Handbooks tend to be heavy borrowers, perhaps on the grounds that by extending knowledge they help repay their debts. This one borrows heavily from six books in particular. Its basic information came from the Canadian Forestry Service's *Native Trees of Canada*, and from Harlow and Harrar's *Textbook of Dendrology*. Provincial tree ranges were found in Roland and Smith's *The Flora of Nova Scotia*. Some of the tree lore was sifted from Dr. William M. Harlow's excellent paperback *Trees of the Eastern United States and Canada*. Certain technical information was taken from the United States Forest Service's *Silvics of Forest Trees of the United States*. Facts about tree pests and diseases came chiefly from the Canadian Forestry Service's *Forest Insects and Diseases of North America*. These and other works consulted are listed in the bibliography. To their authors the writer acknowledges his debt.

INTRODUCTION

Ancient Giants

Look at a tree. It may be no older than you are, but next to ferns, mosses, and lichens it represents the most ancient family of plants now alive on earth. If we were to represent the time span from the beginning of trees till now by a 1,000-page book (i.e., about 6.3 cm or 2.5 in. thick), then the time elapsed since the pyramids were built about 4,000 years ago would be represented in that book by the last line on the last page. To endure so long, trees had to be more than just ordinary members of the vegetable kingdom—and so they are. They are complex, giant plants.

California's huge sequoias may tower more than 107 m (351 ft.) into the sky, and grow to be 9 m (30 ft.) across the butt. To grasp the magnitude of these dimensions, pace them off on the ground. Bristlecone pines of the southwestern United States attain the hoary age of nearly 5,000 years, and our own white pine may reach 450 years. The wood of Central America's lignum vitae is so hard that certain World War II vehicles rolled on bearings made from it. Balsa of South America is so light when dry that an armful weighs only a few kilograms. And many trees, like our balsam fir, are so hardy that they will survive a century of harsh mountain-top weather.

Green Factories

Trees are marvellous factories, too. On a clear hot day an ordinary white elm may suck up and give off 6,819 L (1,500 gal.) of water—a full load for an average tanker truck. Most of this the tree "sweats" through tiny leaf pores, which have shutters to control the rate of evaporation. As in humans, this evaporation prevents overheating, which would kill the leaves. All day the tree inhales through the same pores large quantities of carbon dioxide produced by oxygen-users such as engines, people, wildlife, and bacteria; and all day it exhales life-giving oxygen as a by-product. Night reverses these processes.

Water enters a tree via several hundred kilometres of roots. Rising steadily through a maze of tubes and valves that would baffle any plumber, the mineral-laden water reaches and continually bathes all living tissues in the trunk and crown. To this nutritious water the leaves add air and sunlight to make dextrose, a kind of sugar. From dextrose the tree then builds wood and bark, more leaves and twigs, flowers, seeds, and so on. In other words, a tree is made almost wholly out of water and thin air. No one has yet come close to performing this miracle, though scientists can change wood back into edible sugar.

How Trees Grow

Trees grow as long as they live, but in our latitudes active cell division occurs only during summer. From late May to early August they rapidly produce a crop of leaves, twigs, roots, flowers, seeds, new roots, and a thin layer of new wood and bark over trunk, limbs, and roots. They also grow next year's crop of leaves and flowers, in miniature. Examine a live twig in midsummer. Note how the familiar winter buds are already formed, hidden in the angle above the leaf stem. They contain prefabricated flowers and leaves, all neatly telescoped and fused to burst at the sun's signal next spring.

These same buds are the most helpful feature for identifying leafless trees. Also, from the layers of wood or annual growth rings in the lower trunk we can read the age and much of the life history of the tree.

Winter Preparations

After July or August trees prepare for ice and snow. That means converting dextrose back into various starches and fats for storage in the bark and roots. Usually by the first frost this job is done. The leaf factories are shut down. As certain nutrients are withdrawn from the leaves of deciduous species, hidden colours begin to appear: russet, gold, and scarlet. Soon the leaf stalks are sealed off, and autumn storms strip the trees. Our word "fall" probably comes from this event. The fallen leaves (if not raked away) provide valuable fertilizer for trees, especially nitrogen.

Evergreens do not drop all their needles or markedly change colour in the fall, but they prepare for winter in the same ways.

Thus, well before the snow flies, trees have entered a sort of hibernation or dormancy. In this state they can withstand great cold. On very bitter cold nights, a trunk will sometimes crack with a loud snap, causing a vertical seam which usually heals into a furrow called a frost rib.

Tree Flowers and Seeds

The flowers and seeds of trees deserve special mention. Not only are they interesting in themselves, but they are useful aids in naming unknown species. Tree flowers are mostly tiny—although the fragrant blooms on southern magnolia of the Gulf States may be 20 cm (8 in.) across.

In Nova Scotia, the largest tree flowers occur on apple, cherry, and Juneberry trees. The most obviously colourful are the pink to white blooms of apple, locust, and horse-chestnut trees and the orange-red blossoms of the red maple. On a smaller scale, the claret cone flowers of black spruce and tamarack are strikingly rich in colour. Because most of the native trees depend on wind and not insects to carry the fertilizing pollen, plain little flowers are the rule. These flowers give off such clouds of pollen dust in May and June that the shores of woodland lakes are sometimes yellow with it.

Usually the same tree carries both male and female flowers, as in pines and oaks. Other species such as poplar, willow, and ash bear male and female blossoms on separate trees—one tree is male, the other female. A few tree flowers have the male and female parts combined as in garden flowers. Cherry, elm, and linden trees are of this type. Catkins—drooping flowers that look like caterpillars—are typical of poplar, willow, birch, and alder blooms of both sexes and of the male flowers in oak.

Evergreens such as spruce and fir all bear flowers resembling little cones. The short-lived male flower is found on the lower branch tips; the reddish, often fragrant female flower grows higher up.

Upon fertilization, the core of the female tree flower swells to accommodate the growing seeds. In most trees the seed matures the same year. In some, such as pine and red oak, the process takes two years. Each ripe seed contains a small-scale tree enclosed in enough stored food to get it started in life. Some form of seed-wing is usually provided also, to buoy it on the wind. This gives the seedling a chance to grow outside the full shade of the parent tree. Drop a spruce or elm seed from an upstairs window in a breeze and watch it spin and sail downwind.

Most trees produce bumper crops of seed only every few years. Birds, animals, insects, and disease destroy millions of tree seeds, but normally there are plenty left to provide for young trees.

Leaf-Out

As spring days lengthen, the tree breaks dormancy. The sap stirs again. Stored foodstuffs are changed back to sugar and rushed to the buds in the sweetish and free-running sap. Those who tap sugar maples in March or April take advantage of this. The sugar-laden sap provides fuel to run the tree factory until the leaves can start making their own. Trees run on sugar the way cars run on gasoline, but unlike cars, trees make their own fuel and burn it more slowly. And it is very potent: from winter buds the size of rice grains, a black ash can throw out 40.6 cm(16 in.) leaves in a fortnight.

Once the leaves and flowers are out, it is time for the tree observer to be out as well.

GETTING TO KNOW OUR TREES

Thirty Native Trees

In Nova Scotia there are 30 different kinds of native trees, with softwoods making up about 60 per cent of total volume. Twelve kinds supply all our industrial wood. Counting exotics, or species introduced from other countries, we have about 45 kinds. If we add native and foreign shrubs that reach tree size, the total comes to about 60.

For the purpose of this book, a tree is defined as any self-supporting plant having a single woody stem 3 m (10 ft.), or more, tall. Admittedly this is small for a tree. But it lets us include several kinds of near-trees that are commonly seen and which are sometimes mistaken for larger relatives.

Getting to know several dozen trees may at first seem hard to do. But it is easier than you might think. After all, most of us know and can quickly recognize more than 60 people—and people, as a rule, are more alike than trees. People seem easier to tell apart because they are inherently more interesting.

For those who take the trouble to really look at trees, they can become fascinating objects for summer and winter study. In fact, many people make tree study (or dendrology, from Greek *dendron*, "tree"), a life-long hobby. Others want merely to be able to recognize the trees they come across while walking, working, or travelling. Between these extremes are those whose zeal is less than the hobbyist's but more than the casual onlooker's.

Whatever your interest in trees, you will enjoy taking this guide along wherever new tree species are likely to be encountered: family outings, hunting and fishing expeditions, hiking jaunts, or walks in the local park. And although the booklet describes trees native to Nova Scotia, take it along on out-of-province trips as most of these species range widely over North America. Meeting a familiar tree a thousand kilometres from home is nice.

In our towns, the exotic species most often seen are elm, maple, linden, and poplar, followed by species such as birch, rowan, French willow, horse-chestnut, English and red oak, and black locust. In our forests the common native species are fir, spruce, pine, hemlock, birch, maple, aspen, and oak. More rarely, such native forest trees as hornbeam, witchhazel, and cedar will be encountered.

The first step in getting to know any of them is to group those with common features. This requires a knowledge of those features, so that they can be compared and contrasted to arrive at identities. Then the groups can be split into individual species.

Grouping Trees for Study

All Nova Scotian trees fall into two groups: Needle-leafed (except for one native evergreen, cedar, which has overlapping, scalelike leaves instead of needles, (eg. fir) or broad-leafed (eg. maple). Because needle-leafed species always bear their seeds in cones, hold their leaves for two or more years (except tamarack), and usually have fairly soft wood, they are called conifers, evergreens, or softwoods. Conversely, broad-leafed trees are usually termed hardwoods and described as deciduous (Latin *de cadere,* "to fall off").

LEAF CLUES

If you examine a dozen different needle-leafed trees, you will see that they come in two basic types: those with needles in bundles (eg. pine), and those with needles one by one (eg. spruce). The broad-leafed species also come in two kinds: simple, one-piece leaves (eg. birch), and many-parted or compound leaves made up of several leaflets (eg. ash).

To determine the difference between a compound leaf or a cluster of simple leaves, check the stalk to which they are attached. If it is fleshy, the leaf is compound, if woody, it is simple. After July one can also separate leaflets from true leaves by the presence of a bud at the base of each leaf.

The conifers are easier to learn. Not only do they change little from summer to winter, but there are only 10 of them (unless we count a few exotic species). By learning some individual features of needles, twigs, cones, and bark, one can master them easily. The hardwoods are less easy, and there are three times as many. So we must subdivide them further.

KINDS OF HARDWOOD LEAVES

Of the simple-leafed species there are again two kinds, namely lobed or partly divided as in maple, and unlobed as in birch. Both kinds may have sawlike or toothed edges of varying kinds, which can be quite useful in placing new specimens. Flip through the broad-leaf section of this book and note the several kinds of teeth or serrations. Their purpose may be to shed rain evenly.

Leaf samples taken from saplings or trees in deep shade are apt to be larger than normal and not typical in shape.

Of compound-leafed trees, the native species all have the pinnate form, i.e., with leaflets arranged in a feather pattern (Latin *pinna,* "feather") along a central stalk. The same applies to most of our introduced trees. One exception is horse-chestnut, which has a fingerlike or palmate arrangement of leaflets.

Other leaf features, such as hairiness, vein pattern, texture, and size will be described in the main text.

TWIG CLUES

In winter, hardwoods present a confusing maze of leafless twigs. To many people this makes hardwoods a closed book until the next summer—except perhaps for birch and beech, which they can tell by the bark. Yet hardwood trees are as easy to name in January as in July. Their twigs may look alike at first glance, but a closer look reveals many distinctive features.

Moreover, twig features are more reliable than leaf features. Even on the same tree, leaves vary not only in size, but in shape (no two identical leaves have ever been found), in colour (soil and season affect this), in texture, and in other ways. Certain species are notorious for this leaf variation. Twigs vary too, but not so noticeably.

Twigs come in many colours and kinds: red, yellow, purple, brown, green, and grey; stout and slender; rough and smooth; zig-zag and straight. Some have buds in opposite pairs, others have them alternating or staggered.

Buds also have distinctive qualities. They may be blunt or pointed, large or tiny, shiny or furry. Most are covered by many overlapping shinglelike scales (eg. elm), others by just one scale (eg. willow).

A beech, for instance, has rich brown, spindle-shaped buds. Balsam poplar also stands out in winter because of its large, resinous, aromatic buds. Horse-chestnut is easier still, because it displays the marks of perfect horse-shoes, nails and all, on its stout twigs. The branch pattern of the tree can be helpful in some species, since it reflects the bud pattern of the twigs from which the branches grew.

Splitting the Groups into Species

Having lumped the trees by general features, we can now proceed to split the main groups into species. What follows is a table bringing together the summer features we have been describing. (For softwoods the same features apply in winter.) This table is called a key. This simplified key will ask you for certain facts about the specimen at hand, and then tell you by page numbers where in the book to look for likely candidates. The drawings and descriptions on the pages indicated should soon lead to the correct species.

For twig study, a 10X hand lens and a sharp pen knife are useful.

BROADLEAF TERMINOLOGY

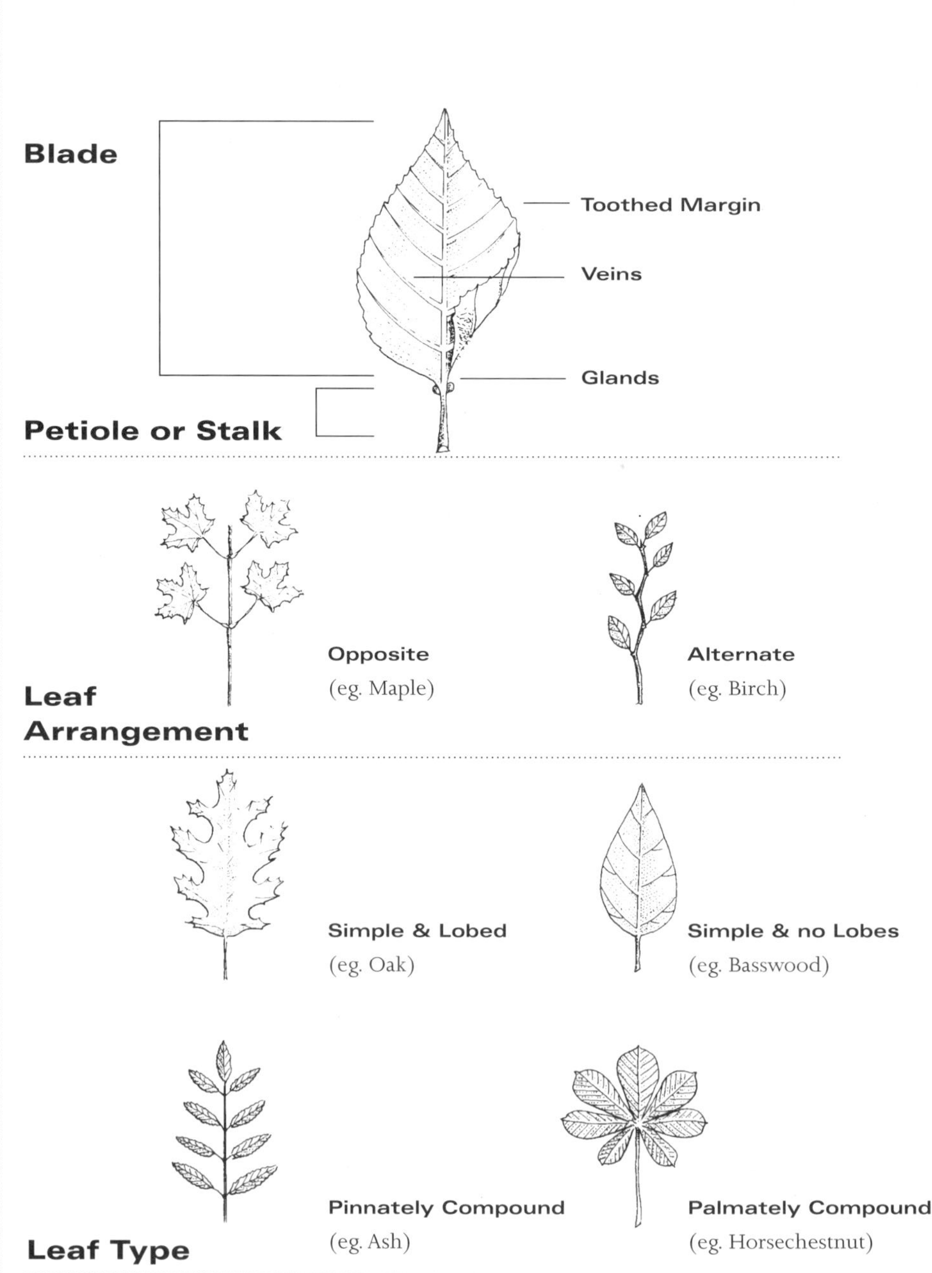

LEAF KEY

Trees with Needlelike or Scalelike Leaves

Needles in bundles
Two needles per bundle 18-20
More than two needles per bundle 16, 22

Needles solitary
Needles flattened 30-34
Needles four-sided 24-28

Trees with Thin, Flat Leaves of Varying Widths

Leaf simple
Leaf lobed 58, 75, 78-84
Leaf unlobed 40-56, 60-70, 74, 91

Leaf compound
Leaf pinnately compound
    Eleven leaflets or fewer 86, 88
    More than eleven leaflets 72, 76, 84, 92
Leaf palmately compound 92

WINTER TWIG TERMINOLOGY

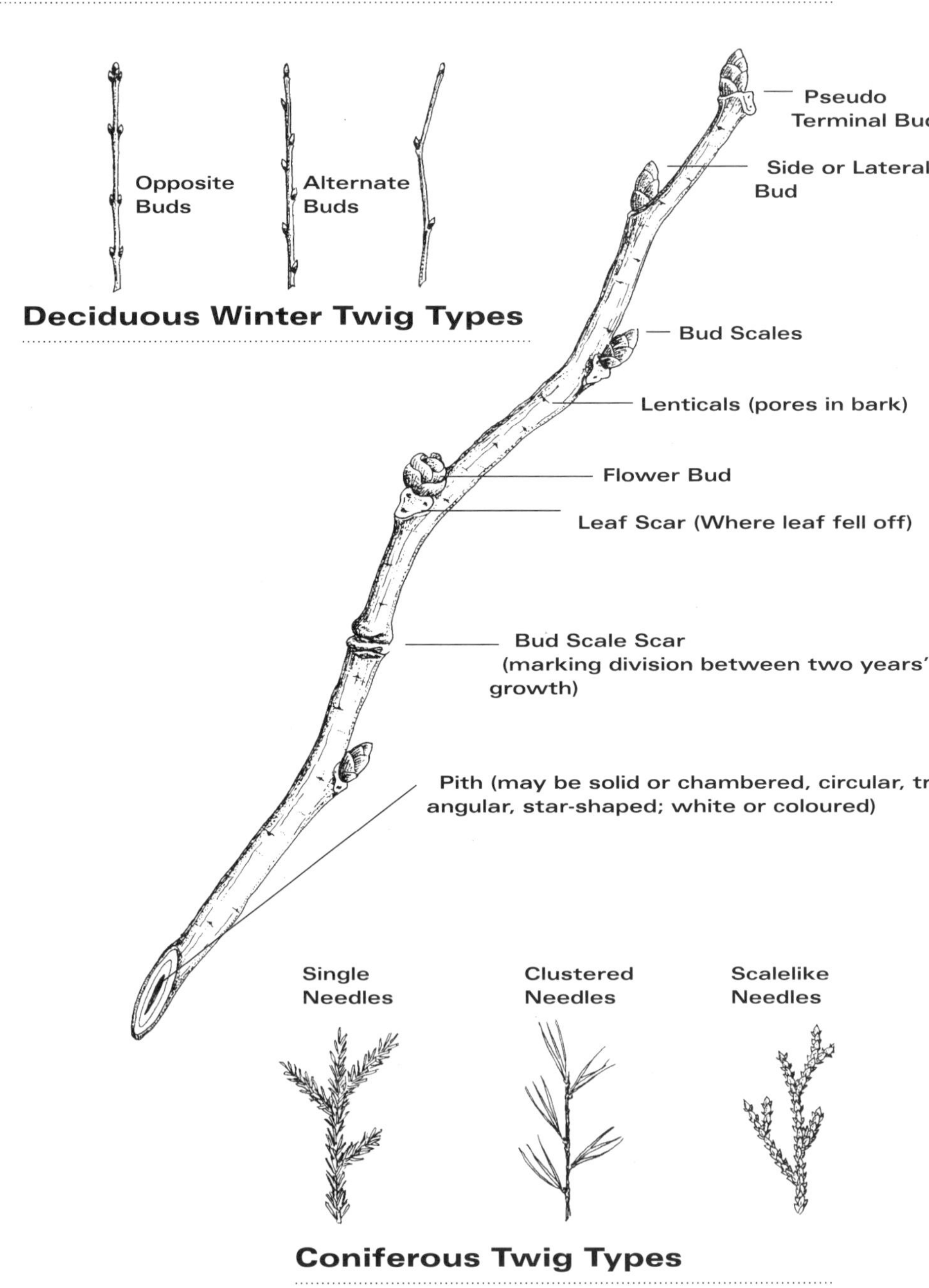

HARDWOOD TWIG KEY

Buds Opposite (Paired)

Leaf scars* with 3 dots only, twig usually reddish to purplish

Buds stalked, with only two visible scales 82,83

    Twigs and buds hairless, bark white-striped 83

    Twigs and buds white-downy, bark not striped 82

Buds not stalked, with several visible scales

    Buds sharply conical 78

    Buds blunt-tipped

    Twig slender, tip bud usually less than 0.5 cm ($\frac{1}{5}$ in.) long ...80, 84

    Twig stout, tip bud usually more than 0.5 cm ($\frac{1}{5}$ in.) long 85

Leaf scars with about 16 dots, twig greenish to greyish 86-90

Leaf scars shaped like horse's hoof print, twigs very stout, buds gummy 92

* Leaf scars are found just under the buds. Each scar marks the place where a leaf stalk parted from the twig the previous autumn. The dots found on the leaf scars of many species are the cut ends of tiny bundles of sap tubes. Because different groups of species have characteristic numbers of bundle-dots, the dots make useful identification features.

SOFTWOODS • INTRODUCTION

Nova Scotia has 10 native softwoods or conifers. In order of volumes present, (as of 1979-89 *Provincial Forest Inventory*) they are: spruce (red and black), balsam fir, white spruce, white pine, hemlock, tamarack, red pine, Jack pine, cedar.

In addition, several introduced species are often seen, notably Scotch pine, Austrian (black) pine, Norway spruce, European larch, and Colorado blue spruce.

Pines are perhaps the best known softwoods. Their bundled needles and large cones set them apart. White pine is of the five-needle or soft pine group, while the other two (plus the introduced ones) are of the two-needle or hard pine group. White and red pine are both important native lumber trees. The foreign pines have been widely planted for reforestation and decoration.

All pines, especially Jack and red pine, do best on sandy soils. In Nova Scotia pines are most plentiful in the western half of the province, becoming scarcer toward Cape Breton. Jack pine, which tends to follow fire and cutting on poor soils, is the smallest and scarcest of the three, white pine the largest and most abundant.

Tamarack is unmistakable among native conifers, with its soft grey-green foliage that turns gold and falls in autumn and its small, rose-shaped cones. This tree keeps company with black spruce on swampy ground, and its wood is the hardest among the native softwoods.

Spruces are our most valuable softwoods because their long-fibred, whitish wood is perfect for making newsprint. Unlike the pines, they have short, single needles. Their cones are smaller too. Red spruce, the most common of the three, is also our most important conifer. Black spruce is usually found in swamps and along the coast, and white spruce (to which Norway and Colorado spruce are similar) has earned the name of pasture spruce by its habit of taking over abandoned farmland.

Hemlock is a graceful tree with shiny needles that are smaller than those of other native conifers. An extract from its rough reddish bark was once used in tanning leather. Since good white pine became scarce, this conifer has become more important for lumber. Look for it on sheltered, moist slopes with pine and red spruce.

Balsam fir is well known as our most popular Christmas tree species. Fir is also Nova Scotia's most common conifer. Though not as valuable as red spruce for timber, it is a major pulpwood species. Its name comes from the clear, aromatic resin found in blisters on the bark.

Cedar is another moisture-loving tree. In Nova Scotia it is very scarce and practically confined to the western counties. The flattened, scalelike needles differ from those of all other native conifers.

WHITE PINE *Pinus strobus* L.

A tall, often spreading five-needle conifer with cigar-shaped tan cones and nearly horizontal upper branches with upcurved tips; the top is often bent permanently to leeward by wind and flattened.

Other common names: Pattern Pine, Yellow Pine, Majestic Pine

This tallest and most stately of eastern softwoods has long been prized in Nova Scotia. After the first sawmilling rig was set up near Riverport, Lunenburg County, about 1632, white pine was eagerly sought and cut, first for home construction, and later for shipbuilding and export.

Since the 1800s, scarcity of large old-growth stands in the province has brought red spruce and other softwoods to the fore as lumber trees. But white pine is still much used here.

This native of the Appalachian and Great Lakes regions is found throughout Nova Scotia but is most common in the western half. It grows in pure stands or mixed with red spruce, hemlock, yellow birch, and sugar maple. Although white pine grows largest in such mixtures—up to 1.2 m (4 ft.) across and 30 m (100 ft.) tall—it is also found on bogs with black spruce and tamarack, and on dry sandy ridges with Jack and red pine, probably as a result of fire. It tolerates some shade. The tree matures in 200 years, but may reach 450.

The tree is threatened by white pine blister rust, a fungus which causes swollen orange-coated branches, abundant resin drippings, a dead top, and eventually death. The spores that infect the pine develop on the leaves of gooseberry and currant bushes (*Ribes* species), and from there they can travel up to 305 m (1,000 ft.) by wind to the nearest white pines. By rooting out all *Ribes* plants within that range, the pines can be protected. Only five-needle pines are susceptible.

The white pine weevil damages leading shoots which results in forked and crooked trunks that are often useless as logs.

White-tailed deer eat the needles and twigs, and red squirrels and crossbills extract the large seeds. Dense young stands make good windbreaks and wildlife cover, but older stands become too open to give much shelter.

NEEDLES

On older twigs in bundles of five (think of
W-H-I-T-E), singly on new shoots; 7.6
cm-12.7 cm (3 in.-5 in.) long; three-cornered; slender; soft; blue green.

CONES

Pendent; longer than those of other native
pines; stalked; cigar-shaped when closed;
resinous; often slightly curved. Scales thin;
bearing two 0.6 cm (^{1}/4 in.) winged
brown seeds that ripen in September of
second year.

TWIGS

Slender; changing from green and downy
at first to orange brown and smooth;
roughened by scars as needles drop; buds
sharp-pointed.

BARK

On young trees smooth; dark green or
brown-tinged (somewhat firlike but without resin blisters); older trunks dark grey
and deeply furrowed into broad up-and-
down ridges. Up to 7.6 cm (3 in.) thick.

WOOD

Highly prized for interior finish. Straight-
grained; even-textured; durable; lightweight;
taking nails, planing, and painting very well.
Sapwood creamy white; heartwood pinkish;
distinctly fragrant. Growth rings faint, but the
dark dots and lines of the resin tubes are easily
seen and serve to separate it from the woods
of red and Jack pine. Air-dry weight about
385 kg/m^3 (24 lb./cu.ft.).

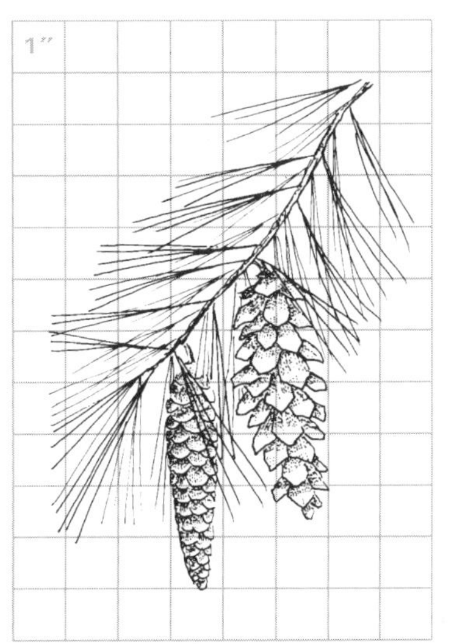

RED PINE *Pinus resinosa* Ait.

A tall, straight, two-needle pine with platy red-brown bark; an open oval crown of tufted appearance; and long yellow-green needles that break cleanly when doubled between the fingers.

Other common names: Norway Pine, Bull Pine

Red pine is only a scattered tree in Nova Scotia, found mainly in sandy and rocky soils on the lowlands of Colchester and Cumberland counties, and in northern Queens and southern Annapolis counties. The natural range of red pine centres on the Great Lakes, but extends from Newfoundland (a few pockets) to southeast Manitoba. It is found both in pure stands and mixed with white or Jack pine. Jack pine tends to replace it after cutting or fire, unless special measures are taken to encourage the red pine seedlings; so this useful species may in time become scarcer.

The sturdy wood and ease of rot-proofing make it ideal for wharf and bridge pilings and hydro poles. Plantations produce valuable logs because natural pruning of lower branches is good in this species, resulting in knot-free lumber. Red pine was once used for ship masts, and the heartwood was selected for ships' decks.

Once valued for plantations, red pine has fallen into disfavour because of the Sirococcus shoot blight, a fungal disease which attacks the shoots and eventually kills the trees. Other damage is done by the European pine shoot moth, the white pine weevil, and the pine root collar weevil.

The name "Norway Pine" may have originated with early Great Lakes voyageurs who mistook it for Old World Norway spruce, or from large stands which grew near the village of Norway, Maine.

In 1971, the *Scleroderris* canker of pines was discovered in New Brunswick. The next year it was found in a 15-year-old red pine plantation in Pictou County. Most pine species are susceptible to attack by this fungus, especially young plantations of red pine and Jack pine in frost-prone areas. Symptoms include yellowing of branch tip foliage and dying of tip buds.

NEEDLES

In twos (also rarely in threes on shoots
infested with grubs of the pine shoot
moth); 7.6-12.7 cm (3 in.-5 in.) long;
dark; shiny, yellow green; straight, not
twisted as in Jack pine. The clean breakage
of needles usually serves to separate red
pine from introduced species such as
Austrian and Scots pine, whose needles are
less brittle.

TWIGS

Stout; rough; orange to red brown; buds
sharp-pointed, resinous, a bit hairy.

CONES

Oval; maturing in two years; small and
upright the first autumn, hanging and
chestnut brown the second, when they
open to release the winged seed; falling the
next spring; scale tips more or less rounded (angled in Scots pine); two seeds per
cone scale; cone not curved or pointed as
in Jack pine.

BARK

Orange brown and flaky on young trees,
later breaking into flat red brown plates.

WOOD

Yellowish to reddish with a pronounced
grain. Lightweight; straight-grained; heavier and harder than white pine; takes cre-
osote very well; has fine dots in growth
rings. Air-dry weight about 448 kg/m^3
(28 lb./cu.ft.).

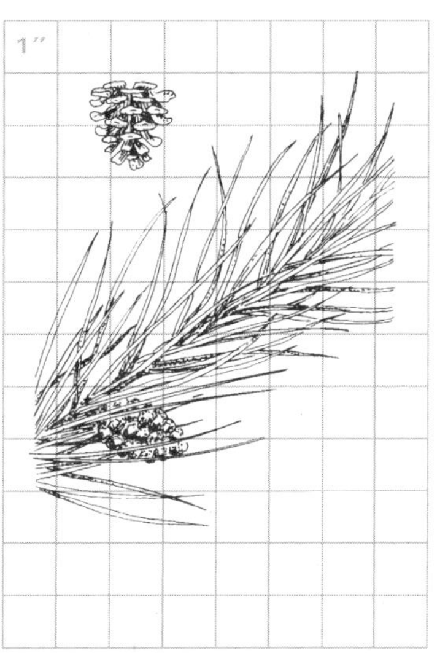

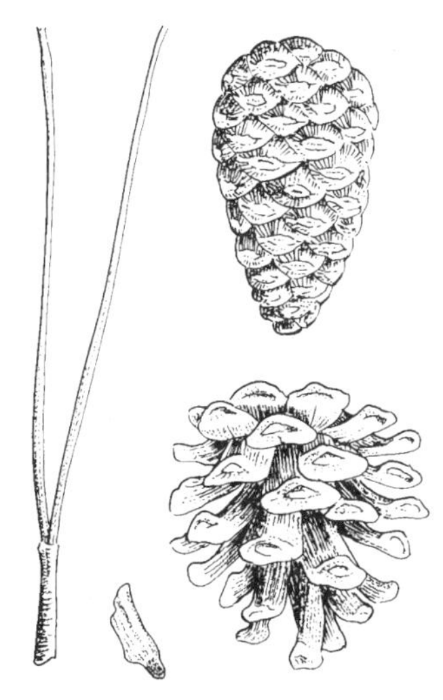

JACK PINE *Pinus banksiana* Lamb

A small to medium-sized two-needle pine of generally ragged outline with twisted yellow-green foliage and curved cones.

Other common names: Princess or Princy Pine, Scrub Pine, Grey Pine

The range of Jack pine is the largest of any native Canadian pine, extending from Cape Breton Island to the Yukon and from the northern tree line to the Lake States. In closed stands on good soils it may reach 24 m (79 ft.) tall and 0.6 m (2 ft.) in diameter. But on poorer and drier sites, where it is commonly found, it seldom exceeds 15 m (49 ft.) tall and 0.3 m (1 ft.) diameter and may be stunted and scrubby.

In Nova Scotia, scattered stands are found on sandy, barren, or ill-drained soils, notably near the isthmus between New Brunswick and Nova Scotia. It is rare in the Annapolis Valley.

Nevertheless, Jack pine may spread in the province because it can take over poor sites recently cleared by fire or cutting, provided seed trees are present. This species usually grows in pure stands, but may be found mixed with black spruce and such post-fire hardwoods as white birch and aspen.

Being scarce and of small size (except in favoured locations), Jack pine is unimportant to our forest industry. Sometimes it is used locally for fuel wood and round timber for rough jobs. In central Canada, where it occurs in extensive pure stands of larger trees, it is used for lumber, railway ties, poles, and kraft pulp (eg. for shopping bags).

Some of the early settlers believed that this pine poisoned the soil—no doubt because of its abundance on poor sites. There was also a superstition among settlers that it was a "witch tree" and not to be tampered with.

Introduced Pines

Scotch or Scots pine (*P. sylvestris* L.) has orange-brown bark; half-round, sharp-pointed needles about 6.3 cm (2^{1}/$_{2}$ in.) long; and tapered 5.1 cm (2 in.) cones. Austrian pine (*P. nigra* Arnold) or black pine has dark green needles about 12.7 cm (5 in.) long. Mugho pine (*P. mugo* Turra var. *mughus* Zenari) is a dwarf form of mountain pine used for ornamental planting. All three are two-needle pines.

NEEDLES

In twos, 1.9 cm-3.8 cm ($^3\!/\!4$ in.-1$^1\!/\!2$ in.)
long, each pair usually twisted and spreading apart; light yellow green; stiff; shorter
than those of other native pines; flattened
(instead of semi-circular or triangular) in
cross-section.

TWIGS

Slender; tough; smooth; yellowish green;
buds reddish brown, rounded.

CONES

Yellowish brown; thick-scaled; maturing
September of the second year (first-year
cones small and oval); usually incurved
toward branch tip; often borne in pairs,
remaining closed on tree for many years
(sometimes even overgrown by branch
wood); bearing two-winged seeds.

BARK

Similar to that of black spruce; thin, reddish brown to dark grey; becoming scaly
and furrowed on old trunks.

WOOD

Creamy white to brownish yellow with
fairly distinct growth rings showing faint
light dots; fairly hard but not strong; fairly
durable under exposure; creosotes well.
Air-dry weight about 496 mg/m^3 (31
lb./cu.ft.).

The distinctive features of the Scotch pine are its orange-brown bark and
twigs; half-round, sharp-pointed needles about 6.3 cm (2$^1\!/\!2$ in.) long; and
its tapered 5.1 cm (2 in.) cones with their raised, angular cone scales.
Austrian or black pine has very dark green needles about 12.7 cm (5 in.)
long. The foliage looks dense and dark at a distance. Mugho pine is used for
ornamental planting only.

TAMARACK *Larix laricina* (Du Roi) K. Koch

A small to medium-sized tree with spirelike, open crown and long straight trunk; soft blue-green deciduous foliage in small clusters resembling whisk brooms; and small upright cones.

Other common names: Juniper, Larch, Hackmatack

Tamarack is unique among native conifers in that each fall it sheds its foliage like a hardwood. It ranges more widely than most conifers—from Newfoundland to Alaska. Its northern limits follow the tree line southward to the Lake States. It is found throughout Nova Scotia, although never abundantly.

A fast-growing tree that tolerates no shade, this species is often forced by shade-tolerant species to inhabit poor open sites, such as peat bogs and swamps. The lowlands of Guysborough County are characterized by mixtures of tamarack, black spruce, and red maple. However it does best on drier sites, where it grows up to 21 m (69 ft.) tall and nearly 0.6 m (2 ft.) in diameter.

During the 1800s, tamarack was so eagerly sought for shipbuilding that the limited stocks of larger trees were depleted. Boatbuilders still use tamarack to make the curved bow piece that fastens to the keel to receive the forward planking.

Today tamarack is cut chiefly for fence posts, poles, and ties. The wood will last over 15 years underground without preservatives.

Rabbits like the needles, while ruffed grouse and other birds eat the seeds. The branchlets are sometimes browsed by deer, and porcupines eat the bark. The tough roots, like those of the spruce, were used by the Mi'kmaq to sew birch bark. The name "juniper" properly belongs to the true juniper (*Juniperus* spp.), a creeping shrub with sharp needles and bluish, berrylike cones.

The worst insect enemy is larch sawfly, which killed whole stands from Nova Scotia to Manitoba around 1900. Moderate to severe infestations of this leaf-eating pest usually persist in Nova Scotia.

Note: A similar tree, European larch (*L. decidua* Mill.), is often planted here. It has yellow-green foliage, larger cones, stout yellowish twigs, and thicker, platy bark.

NEEDLES

Soft; blue green (turning gold and falling in autumn); in clusters of 12 to 30 on older twigs, but singly on new shoots; three-cornered; 1.9 cm-3.2 cm (^{3}⁄4 in.-1 ^{1}⁄4 in.) long.

TWIGS

Orange brown; slender, with numerous short spur shoots after first season, giving them a knobby appearance in winter; buds small, round, dark shiny red.

CONES

Upright; short-stalked; thin-scaled; light brown; resembling a miniature, oblong rose; opening to drop seed the first fall; falling the second season; bearing two winged seeds per fertile scale.

BARK

Thin; in young trees a smooth bluish grey, later red brown and roughened by fine scales.

WOOD

The heaviest and hardest of native softwoods; white to yellow brown and more or less oily; often spiral-grained (i.e., splitting lengthwise in a spiral); quite durable under moist conditions. Air-dry weight about 561 kg/m^3 (35 lb./cu.ft.).

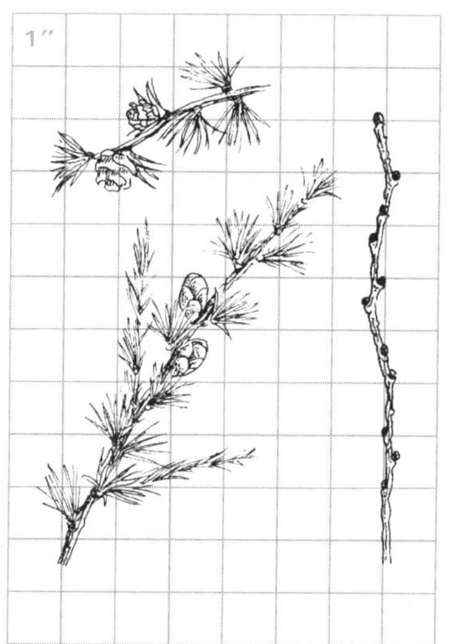

RED SPRUCE *Picea rubens* Sarg.

A medium-sized eastern conifer, normally with dense yellow-green foliage of sharp, four-angled needles, narrow conical crown, reddish scaly bark, and lower branches that usually droop; often hard to tell from black spruce.

Other common names: Spruce, Yellow Spruce, Maritime Spruce

Red spruce, Nova Scotia's provincial tree, is also our most valuable lumber and pulpwood species. Other uses include general construction, boxes and crates, boatbuilding, and ladder stock. On good sites it grows to 28 m (92 ft.) tall and 0.3 m-0.6 m (1 ft.-2 ft.) in diameter. Normally, the trunk is straight and fairly free of dead branches.

After balsam fir, red spruce is our most common softwood, predominating in all but the Cape Breton uplands, and in the western part of the province. Nova Scotia's cool, moist climate is ideal for this tree, and it occurs both in extensive pure stands and mixed with various hardwoods and softwoods.

Though red spruce will grow on swampy soils with black spruce, tamarack, and red maple, it does best on well-drained soils with yellow birch, sugar maple, and beech. Because it interbreeds with black spruce, positive identification is often difficult.

The small branches make a springy mat to place under balsam fir boughs when making a camp bed. (Place the spruce under-side up, the fir face up.) Guitars and other instruments with "spruce" sounding boards usually contain this wood, since it has good resonance properties.

While red spruce can survive in the shade, it requires nearly full light for best growth. This can be seen in the remarkable surge of growth that normally follows release from shade. Under good conditions it reaches saw log size in 60 years, but commonly lives to 200 years (maximum about 400). Spruce budworm, which is mainly a pest of fir, can be a serious enemy where fir forms a large proportion of the stand. Some damage is caused in coastal areas by dwarf mistletoe. Balsam fir sawfly sometimes attacks it; the spruce bark beetle is a serious enemy of old stands; and porcupines like the bark. Windstorms cause some damage because of the shallow roots.

NEEDLES

Four-cornered (to test this, roll one between thumb and forefinger); 1.3 cm-1.6 cm ($^1\!/2$ in.-$^5\!/8$ in.) long; bright yellow green; sharp-pointed; attached to tiny pegs (part of the twig, not of the needle as in fir and hemlock); and growing all around twig with a tendency to curve toward upper side. Generally longer than black spruce needles.

TWIG

Orange brown; slightly hairy; rough when needles removed.

CONES

Pendent; green to purplish green in September; turning reddish brown and opening the first autumn to release two winged seeds per fertile scale; falling in winter. Cone-scale edges nearly smooth (slightly ragged in black spruce, quite smooth in white spruce).

BARK

Finely scaly, thin, reddish brown; inner black brownish yellow.

WOOD

Nearly white to pale yellowish brown; lightweight; straight-grained; fairly strong; grain slightly more pronounced than in white or black spruce. Faint resin tube dots visible in outer parts of growth rings. Without distinctive odour. Air-dry weight about 448 kg/m^3 (28 lb./cu.ft.).

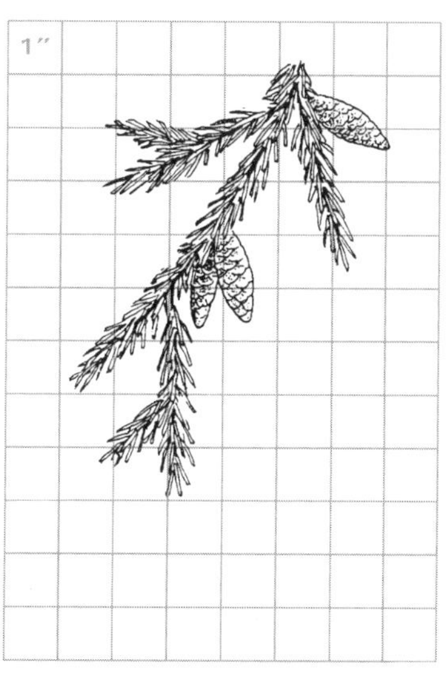

WHITE SPRUCE *Picea glauca* (Moench) Voss

A spirelike, branchy conifer of medium size with ashy-brown, scaly bark, long narrow cones, and sharp four-angled blue-green needles with a rank odour when crushed.

Other common names: Pasture Spruce, Cat Spruce, Skunk Spruce

This species has a North American range slightly exceeding that of tamarack and is the third most plentiful of Nova Scotia's softwoods. Its habit of taking over abandoned farmland (especially in the Annapolis Valley and the lowlands of Cape Breton) is increasing its abundance. The fast-growing white spruce thrives on the moist, well-drained soils along streams and lakes and is common on sandy soils along the coast. Although most commonly found in pure stands, it may occur mixed with other spruces, balsam fir, tamarack, white birch, and aspen.

Pulpwood is its chief use, followed by lumber, boxes, crates, and general construction. Straightness of grain accounts for its use in organ pipes and arrows. Its springiness also makes it useful for scaffolding, ladder rails, and rough flooring. When seasoned, the odourless wood is ideal for food containers.

The Mi'kmaq used its long pliable roots for sewing birch bark on canoes and for decorating baskets. To prepare the slender roots, they steamed coils of them for an hour or so in hot wood ashes, then removed and split them. Just before use, the roots were soaked in hot water.

Although some people use white spruce for Christmas trees, its value is lowered by the rank odour. Moreover, like other spruces, it quickly sheds its needles indoors.

The chief insect enemy of white spruce is the eastern spruce sawfly, which infested some 31,080 km^2 (12,000 sq. mi.) of white and black spruce stands on the Gaspé Peninsula in 1938. Normally, populations of this insect in Nova Scotia are low. Here the spruce budworm and spruce bark beetle do the most damage. The yellow-headed sawfly also does some mild damage. Squirrels sometimes snip off shoots, and porcupines eat the bark.

NEEDLES

Four-cornered; 0.8 cm-1.9 cm ($^1/3$ in.-$^3/4$ in.) long; sharp-pointed; blue green; mounted spirally on little pegs and usually crowding toward upper side of twig; emitting a rank, sometimes unpleasant odour when crushed.

TWIGS

Mostly hairless; orange brown to whitish grey; rough when needles removed.

CONES

Pendent; longer than those of red or black spruce; cone scales completely smooth-edged, bearing two winged seeds each; pale green, turning brown and opening the first autumn; falling in winter.

BARK

Thin; scaly; ash brown to silvery; inner bark streaked with rust brown layers.

WOOD

Nearly white to pale yellow brown, with faint white dots; lightweight; soft; straight-grained; strong in bending; good resonance properties; takes a good finish. Air-dry weight 416 kg/m^3 (26 lb./cu.ft.).

BLACK SPRUCE *Picea mariana* (Mill.) B.S.P.

A small to medium-sized tree with brown, egg-shaped cones, hairy brown twigs, four-angled needles, a straight slender trunk, and a conical crown of short branches, which in older trees droop and carry numerous old cones.

Other common names: Swamp Spruce, Bog Spruce, Red Spruce

Black spruce, a cross-Canada species with a range similar to the white spruce, is fourth in order of abundance among conifers in Nova Scotia. Its main use is for pulpwood (where its denser wood means more usable fibre per cord) and for mine timbers. Where small size is not a limiting factor, it is used in rough construction.

This tree is found throughout the province, but chiefly on poorly drained soils along the Atlantic and Fundy coasts. Its most common associates on the better soils are balsam fir and white spruce, and tamarack on bogland. On exposed bogs or rocky headlands, it survives in low, stunted forms that may be over a century old.

Fishermen use this wood for making lobster traps. They make the curved frame by bending the tough branches into shape, and they saw the laths from specially cut black spruce bolts. Black spruce also yields a good chewing gum.

Black spruce commonly grows new trees by rooting its lower branches in wet moss. It is also one of the first conifers to follow fire, since its sealed cones open best after heat (see Jack pine). The tree matures after about 80 years (maximum 200) of usually slow growth.

The balsam fir sawfly causes a moderate loss of foliage in some locations. Rabbits sometimes destroy seedlings, and porcupines eat the bark. Moose and deer seldom browse it, however.

Introduced Spruces

Of the introduced spruces, the most common are Norway spruce [*P. abies* (L.) Karst.] and Colorado blue spruce (*P. pungens* Engelm.). Both have much larger cones than any of the native species. Also, Norway spruce is distinguished by the drooping habit of its lower branches, and blue spruce by the striking misty blue-green colour of its foliage. Norway spruce is an excellent plantation species as it grows very quickly in Nova Scotia's climate.

NEEDLES

Blue green, 0.6 cm-3.2 cm ($^1/4$ in.-$1^1/2$ in.) long; four-cornered; blunt-pointed on stunted trees; spirally mounted on tiny pegs, sometimes curving to upper side of twig.

TWIGS

Brownish; hairy; otherwise quite similar to those of red spruce.

CONES

Pendent; shorter than in other spruces, with scales always rough-edged; purplish the first winter; borne on the tree for many years both before and after opening.

BARK

Thin; greyish or reddish brown; the inner bark usually olive green (compare red spruce).

WOOD

Nearly white to pale yellow brown, with faint dots in the outer parts of growth rings; denser and stronger than the other spruces 480 kg/m^3 (30 lb./cu.ft.); prone to warping unless very carefully seasoned.

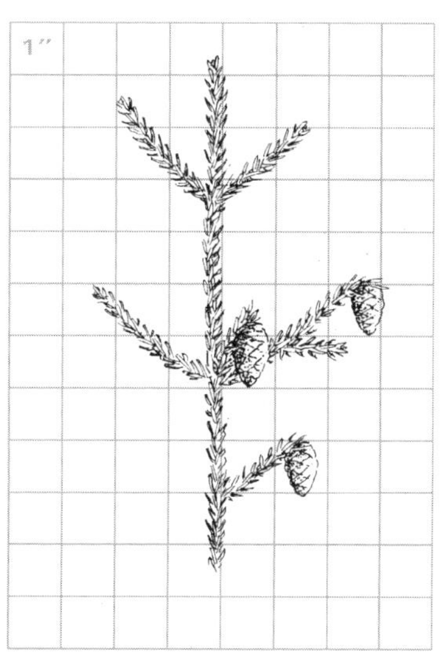

HEMLOCK *Tsuga canadensis* (L.) Carr.

A large conifer with small, glossy, stalked needles; drooping dark green foliage in flat sprays; a leaning tip; and a tapered branchy trunk that develops a deeply furrowed reddish-brown bark.

Other common names: Tree Juniper, White Hemlock

Although we regard hemlock as an important lumber tree, early lumbermen passed it by for the more valuable white pine. Eastern hemlock is not plentiful here, growing mostly in local patches along rich north slopes and ravines, mixed with white pine, red spruce, yellow birch, and sugar maple. However, Queens, Digby, and Annapolis counties once had extensive almost pure stands. Remnants of these remain here and there, with some trees attaining 1.2 m (4 ft.) in diameter at chest height. Today southwestern Nova Scotia has the best hemlock areas in the province.

While hemlock wood can be dressed for interior work, it is more often used for bridge planks, sills, boxes and crates, treated railway ties, culverts, and beams. Because this species retains its lower branches for many years, its wood is usually knotty. These knots probably contain the hardest wood of any eastern tree and can nick an axe blade easily. Hemlock is dangerous in campfires because it throws out sparks.

Young hemlock (often called "white hemlock") are graceful, easy to transplant, and make good ornamentals. Responding well to clipping and trimming, they also produce excellent hedges. An oddity of hemlock is that its main branches grow, not in regular groups or whorls, but in a staggered pattern.

The somewhat similar "ground hemlock" is not true hemlock, but a native yew (*Taxus canadensis* Marsh.). The famous hemlock poison drunk by Socrates came from neither, but from a herb of the *Cicuta* genus.

Early leather-makers leached hemlock bark for tannin, a dye and preservative. Cloth can be dyed a dull red in an extract made from the middle bark. The Mi'kmaq and the early settlers used hemlock for a variety of medicinal purposes.

Hemlock looper damages foliage in certain areas of the province. Deer and rabbits browse hemlock when other food is scarce. Porcupines gnaw the bark.

NEEDLES

Dark, shiny green and flattened, with two
white lines below; 0.8 cm-1.7 cm ($^1/3$ in.-
$^2/3$ in.) long; blunt-tipped and two-ranked
like balsam fir, but borne on short slender
stalks that come off with the needles—a
feature not shared by any other eastern
conifer.

TWIG

Slender; hairy; brownish, with tiny blunt
buds.

CONES

Similar to those of tamarack, but longer
and not erect; pale green with slightly
toothed scale margins, each fertile scale
bearing two winged seeds; cone turning
red brown at maturity; opening when dry,
closing when wet; falling during early
winter.

BARK

Reddish or greyish brown; changing with
age from scaly or flaky to rough and
deeply furrowed; inner bark with purplish
to cinnamon streaks; rich in tannin (11 per
cent).

WOOD

Buff with a reddish tinge; tough and splin-
tery; fairly hard; annual rings distinct;
inclined to be cross-grained and to twist in
seasoning; said to be rat-proof. Air-dry
weight about 464 kg/m^3 (29 lb./cu.ft.).

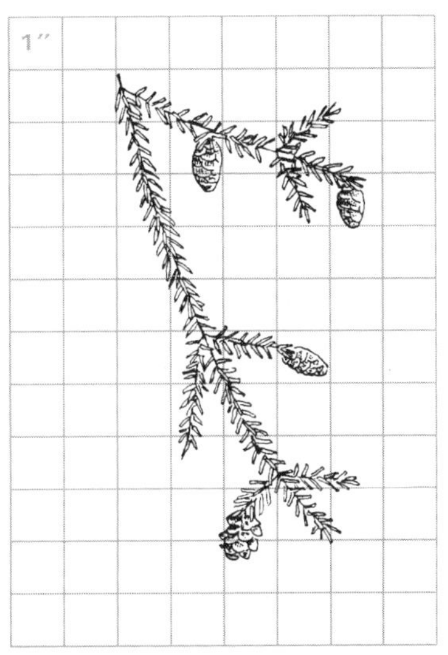

BALSAM FIR *Abies balsamea* (L.) Mill.

A dense steeple-shaped conifer of small to medium stature, with prominent resin blisters on smooth grey-brown bark; flat unstalked needles; and upright dark purple cones.

Other common names: Fir, Balsam, Var

Thriving best in a damp climate, balsam fir is common throughout the Maritimes, especially on the Cape Breton uplands. It grows to around 18 m (59 ft.) tall and 0.3 m-0.6 m (1 ft.-2 ft.) in diameter, and matures in 60 to 70 years (maximum around 150).

Fir is a valuable softwood, excelled here only by spruce for pulpwood. It has some lumber uses. Many Nova Scotia landowners now cultivate it profitably for Christmas trees. Cultivation includes weeding and thinning natural stands and shaping individual trees.

The clear, oily resin ("Canada balsam") is used to make glass cement for microscope slides because it bends light to the same degree as glass. Pioneers used balsam to heal sore throats, and woodsmen still apply it as a stopgap dressing for cuts.

Fir grows best on moist, well-drained loams, but adapts itself to cold swamps and rocky exposed headlands, where it usually becomes stunted. At high elevations it may not even look like fir, with its gnarled trunk twisting along the ground for protection and its boughs flattened by gales and storms.

This species can survive several decades of shading by other trees and still respond quickly when the shade is removed. It is found either in pure stands, or mixed with white pine, the spruces, tamarack, hemlock, birch, aspen, and maple. Its vigorous, deep-rooted seedlings tend to replace those of the more valuable spruce after cutting. The fir is short-lived, however. Various insects and diseases will attack it after 40 or 50 years, especially on drier sites.

There are two chief insect enemies. The balsam woolly aphid, which may blanket the bark, can deform or kill whole stands in a few years. The spruce budworm is a small needle-eating caterpillar, which prefers fir. Defoliation for five years or more in a row kills the trees.

Deer and moose browse the foliage heavily. Porcupines girdle many trees. The seeds are eaten by several bird species, including ruffed grouse.

NEEDLES

Found along opposite sides of twiglike
oars on a racing shell (spruce has bottle-
brush arrangement) 1.9 cm-3.8 cm ($^3/4$
in.-1$^1/2$ in.) long; dark shiny green above,
two white lines below; blunt-tipped or
notched (spruces more or less sharp); fragrant when crushed or dried.

CONES

Upright; dark green to purple, often with
whitish resin droplets; ripening about
October and falling apart, leaving erect,
naked centre spikes ("candles"). (Spruce
cones hang down, and fall whole after
maturity.) Seed purplish, two per cone
scale.

BARK

On young stems a smooth dull green, later
with greyish patches and numerous raised
resin blisters to 3.8 cm (1$^1/2$ in.) wide.
Mature stems red brown; slightly scaly;
breaking into small plates on old trees.

WOOD

Creamy white; soft; light; weaker, less
durable in dampness than spruce or pine;
can be separated from the similar spruce
by absence of tiny white dots (resin tubes)
in dark part of annual ring. Air-dry weight
about 385 kg/m^3 (24 lb./cu.ft.). (Density
about 20 per cent lower than for black
spruce.)

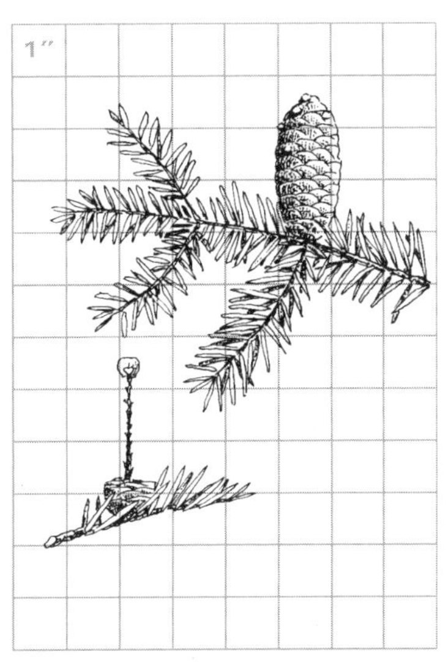

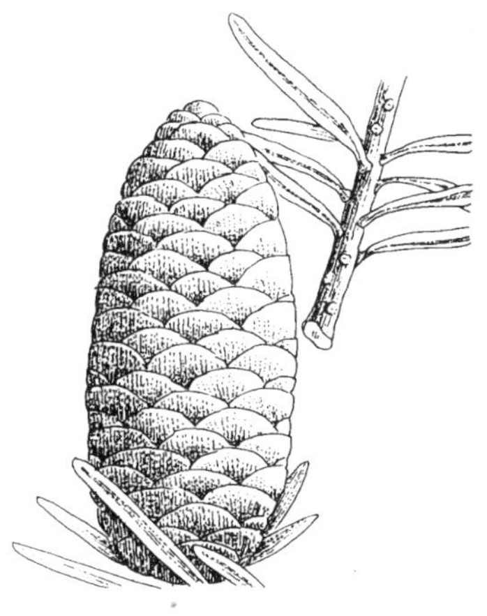

CEDAR *Thuja occidentalis* L.

A small conical tree with scalelike, overlapping leaves that produce dense, dark yellow-green foliage, which often looks clipped or pruned; shreddy brown bark; and a much-tapered trunk.

Other common names: Northern White Cedar, Arbor-vitae

Except as an ornamental, cedar is too rare to be important in Nova Scotia. Its natural range is around the Great Lakes and east through New Brunswick and New England, with pockets as far south as North Carolina. The decay-resistant wood is used for fence posts and shingles. Cedar is also favoured in canoe construction, where strength, lightness, and freedom from warping and decay are essential. Its rubbery toughness is remarkable—a folded cedar shaving can be struck repeatedly with a hammer without breaking.

The local range is virtually confined to the western end of Nova Scotia, such as in back regions of Digby and Yarmouth counties, where it is found scattered around swamps, lakes, and springs. On the Chignecto isthmus there is a slight "spill-over" from New Brunswick, the only Atlantic province where the species is common. Cedar has been widely planted as an ornamental and apparently has escaped in some places to form local stands. This has happened in parts of the Annapolis Valley.

Arbour-vitae is Latin for *l'arbre de vie* (tree of life). This name is said to have been given to the tree by the king of France about 1535, when explorer Jacques Cartier brought specimens to him from the New World. Thus, cedar may have been the first North American tree introduced into Europe. Cartier's men are said to have been cured of scurvy by medicine that aboriginal people made for them by steeping the twigs. The dry outer bark was also shredded and used as tinder.

Deer browse the branches heavily in winter. Rabbits eat the foliage and gnaw the bark of young trees.

North America's two *Thuja* species are not true cedars. The true cedars of antiquity, such as the Biblical "cedars of Lebanon," belong in the genus *Cedrus*, which has evergreen leaves of larchlike form.

NEEDLES

Very small—about 0.3 cm ($^1/8$ in.) long;
pointed; flattened; overlapping in opposite
pairs; and tightly covering the twiglike
shingles; dull yellow green.

CONES

Erect; oblong; composed of four to six
pairs of thin brown scales; maturing in late
summer; opening and remaining on tree
over winter. Seeds small (716,625/kg or
325,000/lb.), two and sometimes three
per scale, with narrow wing along each
side.

TWIGS

Slender; flattened; bearing flat, fan-shaped
sprays; buds minute, scaleless, covered by
needles.

BARK

Thin; fibrous; reddish to greyish brown;
the inner bark tough enough to make into
string or rope.

WOOD

The lightest and most decay-resistant of
eastern woods, yet tough under impact;
pale brown to nearly white with a pleasant
fragrance; soft (a sharp blade cuts it much
like cheese); brittle; low shrinkage. Air-dry
weight 336 kg/m^3 (21 lb./cu.ft.).

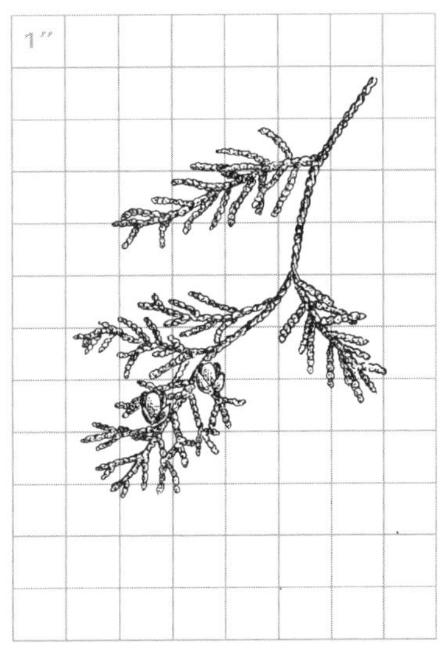

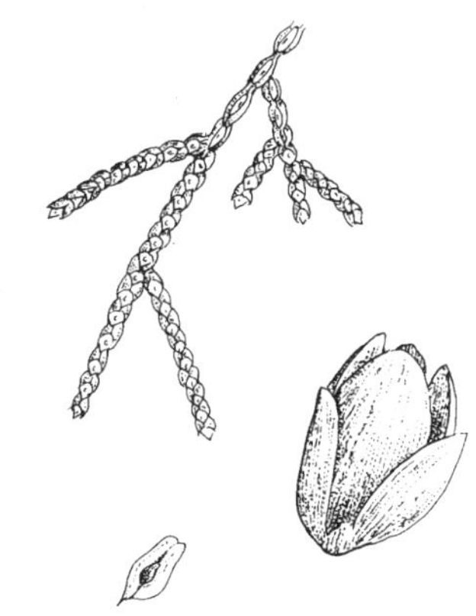

HARDWOODS • INTRODUCTION

Nova Scotia has 14 native hardwoods of greater or lesser commercial importance. In order of volumes present (as of *1979-89 Provincial Forest Inventory*), the principal ones are: red maple, sugar maple, yellow birch, white birch, aspen, beech, red oak, white ash, grey birch, black ash, ironwood, and American elm.

Other native noncommercial hardwoods that reach tree size are: red ash, speckled alder, witchhazel, mountain-ash, mountain maple, striped maple, sumac, pin cherry, black cherry, choke cherry, serviceberry, willow, and hawthorn.

The introduced hardwoods most commonly seen are: linden, Norway maple, sycamore maple, Manitoba maple, silver maple, Scotch elm, English elm, Chinese elm, apple, horse-chestnut, black locust, European ash, European birch, Carolina poplar, Lombardy poplar, silver poplar, English oak, willow, plum, and cherry. These exotics will be described briefly with their native relatives.

Our list includes nearly 50 different broad-leafed trees. A few notes will help to introduce the more important groups.

Aspens prefer moist, sunlit ground in forest clearings and on new burns. They are noted for drooping catkins, prolific sprouting, and leaves that tremble almost constantly. Poplars are close cousins, but have sticky buds and heavier seed capsules.

Willows and aspens are closely related, as their catkins reveal. Most willows have narrow leaves, and many have colourful twigs. They thrive near water. Only a few reach tree size.

Birches are handsome trees, known chiefly by their papery bark. White and grey birch often come up in pure stands after fire. Yellow birch is our most important hardwood.

Beech has the best bark in which to carve initials—though the practice is bad for the tree. Its spine-covered, three-cornered nuts are also well known. The native species grows in hilly parts of the province. Imported beech are seen here and there in provincial towns.

Oaks, like maples, have lobed leaves. Northern red oak is our only native oak. The bristles on its leaf quickly set it apart from other oaks. A forest tree, it is not plentiful in this province.

Elms have only a single native species in Nova Scotia—American elm. This big, umbrella-shaped tree with lopsided, sandpapery leaves is seen mostly along rivers. In the early 1900s, American elm was also widely planted in the Maritimes' towns as a shade tree. Imported relatives are the Scotch and English elms.

Maples are well-known trees of forest and town. All have lobed opposite leaves that take on striking colours every fall, a feature that accounts for their popularity as ornamentals. From this group comes Canada's national emblem. Sugar maple is famed for syrup and fine wood.

Ash is the only large native tree with compound leaflets. If found in a swamp it will likely be black ash; elsewhere in the forest it is safe to call it white ash. Red ash is rare here.

TREMBLING ASPEN *Populus tremuloides* Michx.

A small to medium-sized slender tree with pale greenish-brown bark, fine-toothed roundish leaves that flutter in the least breeze, and shiny brown twigs with sharp buds.

Other common names: Poplar, Popple, Quaking Aspen

Trembling aspen, though common across the province, is not an important timber tree locally. Floors made from it wear to a beautiful, splinter-free white, but sugar maple is more durable. At present its chief uses are veneer and mouldings. Other uses are chemical pulp, excelsior, boxes, toys, and baskets.

It is important as a "nurse crop" for more valuable species. After fire or cutting, this short-lived poplar is often among the first trees to appear, arriving by windblown seeds or by root suckers and stump sprouts. Under its shade, slash decays rapidly, and the seedlings of softwoods and other shade-tolerant trees soon develop. In 20 to 30 years these seedlings crowd out the aspen, leaving only scattered survivors, which may live to 80 or 90 years. Aspen leaf-fall helps to lower soil acidity.

The long hairs on the seeds buoy them up and enable them to travel for miles on air currents. Water also spreads the seeds.

Root suckers arise from root buds 10 cm or 13 cm (4 in. or 5 in.) below the surface. The root buds are stimulated by the increased sunlight and heat reaching the ground after fire or cutting.

Trembling aspen sometimes reaches a height of 21 m-24 m (69 ft.-79 ft.) and a diameter of 0.3 m-0.6 m (1 ft.-2 ft.). More often it is 12 m-15 m (39 ft.-49 ft.) tall and less than 0.3 m (1 ft.) in diameter. Though forming extensive pure stands, it also mixes with other pioneer species such as large-tooth aspen, white birch, and pin cherry.

Aspen provides important wildlife forage. Moose and deer feed on the leaves and twigs; ruffed grouse eat its winter buds; rabbits and mice like the bark and twigs; and beavers make the bark their staple diet.

The major enemies of aspen in Nova Scotia are hypoxylon canker, which kills the bark, and the leaf-eating forest tent caterpillar.

LEAVES

Simple; alternate; lustrous dark green above, dull yellow green below; borne on a vertically flattened stem about as long as the leaf is wide.

TWIGS

Slender; shiny, reddish brown with a star-shaped pith; buds shiny dark brown, mostly sharp-pointed and incurved toward twig.

SEEDS

Minute; released from 0.6 cm (^{1}/4 in.) greenish capsules to float downwind on silky "parachutes."

FLOWERS

Opening before the leaves from special large buds in drooping hairy spikes or catkins (i.e., "little cats"); composed of hundreds of tiny blooms without petals; male and female catkins on different trees.

BARK

Smooth and pale on young trees; becoming furrowed and dark brown or grey.

WOOD

Soft; light; not strong; white to grey brown; not durable when left exposed; takes and holds nails well, and can be nicely finished; inclined to warp unless piled correctly while drying; milled stock tends to have fuzzy edges; and the wood has a faintly rancid odour when wet. Air-dry weight about 448 kg/m^3 (28 lb./cu.ft.).

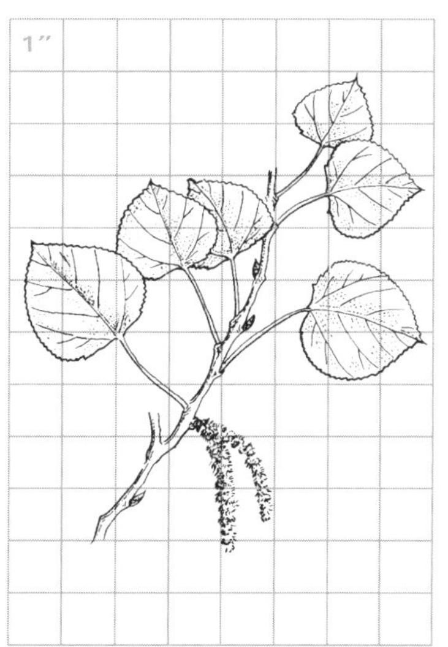

LARGETOOTH ASPEN *Populus grandidentata* Michx.

A small to medium-sized tree with coarse-toothed, trembling leaves, olive-green to brownish bark, downy twigs and buds, and catkins in spring.

Other common names: Poplar, Bigtooth Aspen

Largetooth aspen is a tree of eastern North America and is found across Nova Scotia on light soils or burnt-over sandy areas. It is especially plentiful in the Annapolis Valley. Because the seeding habits and light needs of trembling and largetooth aspen are similar, they often grow together. However, largetooth aspen seems to need a sandier soil than its counterpart. Sandy slopes and stream banks in particular are preferred. Other common associates are white birch, grey birch, and pin cherry.

The wood is not much used commercially. Like that of trembling aspen, it is made into core veneer, matches, boxes, and sometimes firewood. In other parts it is also used in chemical pulp. As wildlife forage, it serves the same needs as trembling aspen. Sometimes the logs of both are stained with a preservative and used in log cabin construction. Their softness makes for easy notching and fitting with only axe and saw. For the same reason both aspens are commonly used for rustic camp and cottage furniture.

Largetooth aspen is fast-growing and short-lived, commonly sprouting from the stump. The seeds are wafted long distances by wind and carried by water. Like those of trembling aspen, they germinate within a day or two after alighting on moist ground. Bare soil is preferred. Few seedlings survive to maturity, however, the main form of reproduction is by root suckers. Like the willows, both aspens are said to root and grow well from fresh cuttings stuck into moist ground.

The forest tent caterpillar is sometimes a serious pest. Hypoxylon canker damages younger trees. The leaves are sometimes infected with a minor disease called ink spot.

LEAVES

Dark green above, paler below; borne on vertically flattened stalks that result in almost constant fluttering; alternate; simple.

TWIGS

Stouter than trembling aspen, with larger buds; twigs and buds more or less grey-downy but can be hairless; pith star-shaped.

FLOWERS

Male and female on separate trees in drooping, hairy catkins; appearing before the leaves.

SEEDS

Minute; silken-haired; contained in 0.3 cm-0.6 cm (^{1}/8 in.-^{1}/4 in.), pale, downy green capsules arranged on loose catkins and developing with the leaves; the capsules splitting when ripe.

BARK

Smooth and olive green at first, becoming brownish and furrowed (almost black at base of old trees).

WOOD

Whitish to pale brown; soft; lightweight; not strong; prone to decay unless kept dry; recognizable as aspen by fuzzy edges in milled stock, but usually inseparable from trembling aspen. Air-dry weight about 448 kg/m^3 (28 lb./cu.ft.).

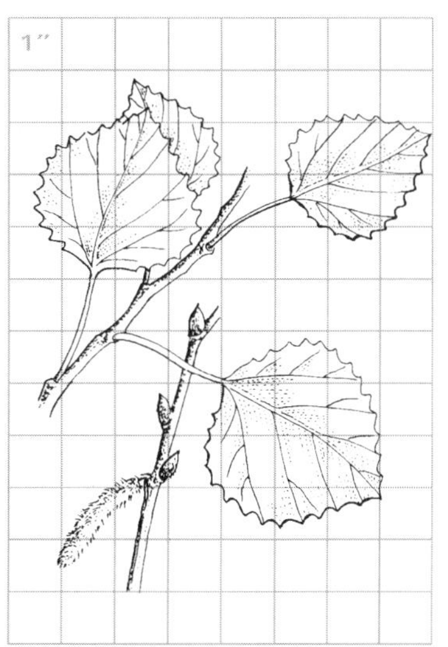

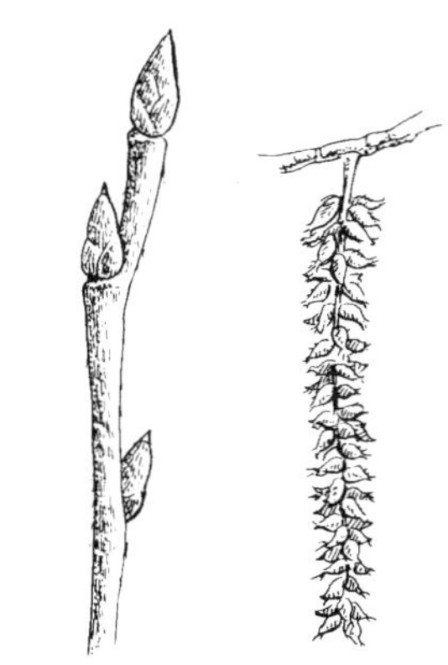

BALSAM POPLAR *Populus balsamifera* L.

A medium-sized tree bearing somewhat heart-shaped leaves with rusty blotches underneath; stout twigs with large, sticky, aromatic buds; and long fluffy catkins in spring.

Other common names: Balm of Gilead, Black Poplar

This native poplar is scarce in Nova Scotia. It is rarely seen as a native forest tree outside of northern Cape Breton, and there it is not plentiful. However, balsam poplar does occur in pockets across Canada, in the northwestern mountains of the United States, and in Alaska. It will grow on all but the wettest and driest sites, but the most favoured habitat is rich bottomlands. Here it forms small pure stands, or mixes with willow, alder, white birch, fir, and spruce. Like the aspens, it shuns shade.

Many settlers planted the balsam poplar around their homes, where its descendants can often be found today. The tree matures in about 100 years but may live for 200. From its resinous buds and those of a very similar species (see note below), a compound is extracted that effectively stops bleeding from minor cuts, and which, when used in an inhalator, clears cold-clogged nasal passages. This is sold under various trade names, notably "Friar's Balsam."

This poplar has no commercial value in Nova Scotia. As an ornamental it is not highly valued either because its catkins litter the ground in late spring, and its gummy buds attract wasps. On the prairies, however, planted rows of it serve as valuable windbreaks. The wood is used for veneer, lumber, excelsior, fuel wood, and pulp. Sometimes the tree is set out as a nurse crop in white spruce plantations.

Fire quickly kills the young trees. The forest tent caterpillar will eat the leaves if aspen leaves are scarce.

Note: Balsam poplar can be confused with a similar poplar called Balm-of-Gilead (P. *candicans* Ait.), which is occasionally found in western counties. The only difference between them is that the leaves of the latter are hairy, especially on the veins beneath. According to Roland and Smith, Balm-of-Gilead may be a cross between balsam poplar and some European species.

LEAVES

Dark glossy green above with rusty blotches below; hairless; base rounded; stalk not
flattened; alternate; simple.

TWIGS

Stout, shiny red brown twigs with large
aromatic buds that exude an aromatic resin
("balm"); pith star-shaped.

FLOWERS

Long drooping fluffy catkins; male and
female on different trees; appearing before
the leaves.

SEEDS

Minute; tufted; contained in 0.6 cm ($^{1}/_{4}$
in.) brown capsules on long, loose catkins;
early summer.

BARK

Smooth greenish to brownish at first,
becoming dark grey and deeply furrowed.

WOOD

Very similar to that of the aspens, except
with a greyish tinge. Air-dry weight about
464 kg/m^3 (29 lb./cu.ft.).

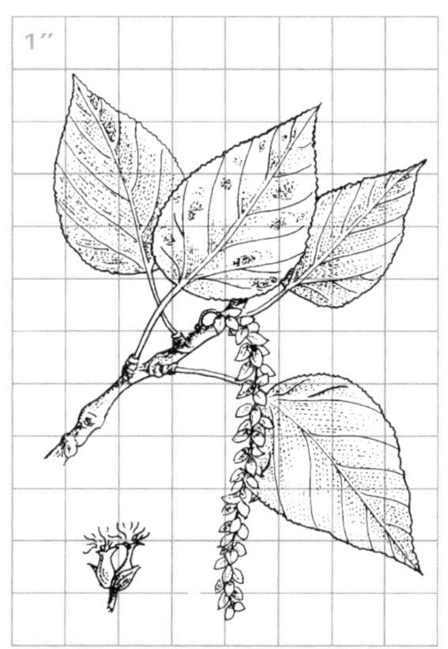

INTRODUCED POPLARS

Three introduced poplars are commonly seen planted about homes and streets: Carolina poplar, Lombardy poplar, and white poplar. Each is easy to tell from the others in summer and in winter.

The first two are hybrids, i.e., cross-bred types not able to reproduce by seed; therefore, each descended, by means of cuttings, from a single original parent. Both the hybrids have flattened leaf-stalks like our aspens. Unlike our aspens, they have a translucent leaf edge.

Carolina Poplar P.X. *canadensis* Moench

A tall tree with upswept branches; bright green, glossy, triangular leaves that flutter audibly in the least breeze; curved yellowish twigs; and drooping catkins (male only). Fast-growing; handsome; resistant to smoke and dust, but not recommended for street planting because the roots seek out and crack water and sewer mains. If Carolina poplar is to be destroyed on this account, the bark should be girdled in spring and the tree not removed until fall, to prevent suckering. Also called "hybrid poplar" locally. One of its original parents was probably Lombardy poplar.

Lombardy Poplar P. *nigra* L. var *italica* Muenchh.

A medium-sized to tall tree easily recognized by its narrow, spirelike crown of small, sharply upcurved branches; dark green triangular leaves that flutter as above; slender, curved, yellowish twigs; and dark grey, furrowed bark. Very decorative, but in our climate it is short-lived and subject to damage from sleet, insects, and disease.

White Poplar P. *alba* L.

A small, branchy tree with wavy-edged leaves that are dark green above and felty white beneath (making the tree appear suddenly silvery when a gust of wind turns the leaves); downy-white twigs and buds, and dark grey, furrowed bark. The common variety *nivea* has a maplelike,  lobed leaf, and is often mistakenly called "silver maple." (The true silver maple has the leaves silvery-smooth beneath.) Once established, this tree is very hard to get rid of due to its abundant and vigorous root suckers.

WILLOW *Salix* spp.

There are over a dozen native and introduced willows which sometimes reach tree size. All are variable in their features, and many interbreed. In general they have narrow leaves and colourful, flexible twigs with numerous alternate, one-scaled buds that press close against the twig. For detailed information consult one or more of the publications on Nova Scotia plants listed in the References.

The only two that reach the stature of large trees are the introduced French or golden willow [*Salix alba* var. *vitellina* (L.) Stokes] and crack or brittle willow (*S. fragilis* L.). French willow is the more common. The introduced weeping willow (*S. babylonica* L.) is smaller and distinguished by its lovely crown of narrow leaves borne on slender drooping branchlets.

Both have glossy, narrow, lance-shaped leaves that taper to the base. Those of French willow usually have the midrib slightly hairy beneath. In crack willow the midrib is hairless. The best distinction, however, is that crack willow branchlets break away very easily and cleanly at the base when bent sharply downward (hence the name), but those of French willow do not.

Both willows were introduced from Europe, where with other *Salix* species, they are important for basketry.

YELLOW BIRCH *Betula alleghaniensis* Britton

A medium-sized tree with yellowish curly bark (almost black in old age); oblong sharp-pointed leaves; and a wintergreen taste to its twigs.

Other common names: Curly Birch, Hard Birch, Black Birch

Yellow birch is our second most valuable hardwood (after sugar maple) and the largest of our native birches. It comprises nearly 15 per cent of our hardwood stock, while sugar maple comprises about 23 per cent of the total. It is found everywhere in the province, especially in the upland hardwood mixtures of the Musquodoboit, Pictou, and Cape Breton hills and the Cobequid Mountains.

On these uplands its most common associates are sugar maple, red maple, beech, red spruce, hemlock, and balsam fir. Yellow birch prefers cool northern slopes, but in the central counties it also occurs on swampy land. Around the coast it is scarce.

It ranges from Newfoundland west to Minnesota, and south through the Appalachians to the northeast corner of Georgia. It may grow to about 21 m (69 ft.) tall and 0.6 m (2 ft.) in diameter. In favourable conditions it lives about 300 years.

In the 1700s, yellow birch was popular with shipbuilders for its durability, especially for those parts of the ship that were underwater. Today we use yellow birch for flooring, furniture, doors, veneers and plywood, cabinet work, and basket-making. A handful of the oily bark shreds will start a fire even on a rainy day, and oil of wintergreen (used to flavour medicine) can be distilled from the bark. The presence of this oil makes the tree easily damaged by fire. Yellow birch is a favourite browse of deer. Many birds eat the seed, and grouse eat the buds and catkins.

Yellow birch is often found growing "on stilts," with open space between the roots and ground. This happens when a seed sprouts and takes root on a rotting stump or log that later crumbles away. Cracks in boulders are another prime place. Bare mineral soil is best of all.

Natural enemies are birch dieback, bronze birch borer, and white-marked tussock moth.

LEAVES

Dark glossy green above, yellow green below; usually hairless; alternate; simple.

TWIGS

Slender; brownish; smooth or hairy; more or less zig-zag; with a 0.6 cm ($^1/4$ in.) long, chestnut brown fuzzy.

FLOWERS

Greenish; male in clustered catkins that elongate in spring from catkins formed the fall before; female much smaller, solitary; appearing from special buds with the leaves; both on same twig.

SEEDS

Tiny, two-winged nut borne by hundreds in an egg-shaped 2.5 cm-3.8 cm (1 in.-$1^1/2$ in.), upright cone; ripening in autumn; shed during fall and winter; cone sometimes present all winter.

BARK

On young trees thin, smooth, yellowish brown; soon developing thin papery curls; on very old trunks thick, platy, and reddish brown to nearly black.

WOOD

Highly prized for its strength, hardness, handsome figure, and fine finishing qualities, in all of which it excels white birch; pale yellow to reddish brown. Air-dry weight about 705 kg/m^3 (44 lb./cu.ft.).

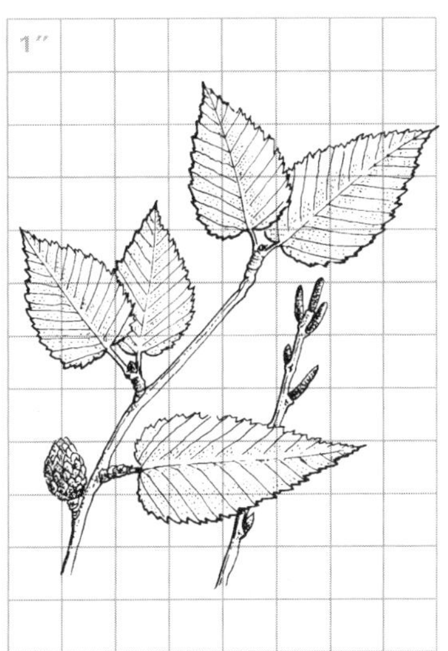

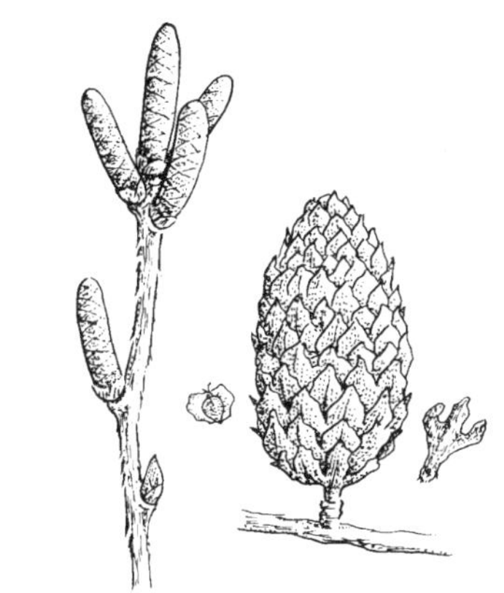

WHITE BIRCH *Betula papyifera* Marsh.

A medium-sized tree with chalky white, easily peeled, papery bark, more or less heart-shaped leaves, and catkins.

Other common names: Paper Birch, Canoe Birch, Silver Birch

White birch is common across Nova Scotia, especially near the Bay of Fundy and eastward. Mostly it is found scattered among softwood growth. But sometimes large pure stands are formed, especially where fire has bared the mineral soil on moist sites. Because its bark is thin and very flammable, fire is also one of its worst enemies.

Typical associates are aspens, willows, and pin cherry, which also prefer mineral soil and open sunlight. Like them, it is fast-growing and short-lived (60 to 75 years). Eventually all but the tallest die from the shade of the longer-lived, shade-tolerant softwoods which in time overtop them. These scattered lone trees are especially noticeable on pulpwood cutovers, where the removal of softwoods and the sudden influx of sunlight and heat usually kill them.

White birch will sprout from the stump (called "coppice growth") after fire or cutting, and in this way whole stands may regenerate in clumps. It grows up to 21 m (69 ft.) tall and 0.8 m (2.5 ft.) in diameter.

Products from this species include veneers and plywood, spoolwood, clothespins, handles, dowels, toys and woodenware, railway ties, and barrel hoops. Much is cut for firewood also. Aboriginal people fashioned the famed birch bark canoe (whose design Europeans later copied in cedar and canvas), rain-tight wigwams, cook pots, cups, and plates from white birch. Settlers put it under their shingles, and it has long been used to kindle campfires.

Refrain from peeling the bark off live trees. Removing more than the top few layers causes the inner bark to turn black and unsightly.

In the early 1900s, a mysterious disease called birch dieback began to destroy vast areas of birch in eastern North America. No explanation was found. About 1940 it reached Nova Scotia. However, since about 1950, the trouble seems to have subsided. Other enemies include the bronze birch borer and the birch leaf skeletonizer.

LEAVES

Smooth dark green above, paler and slightly
hairy below; alternate; simple; the base varying from heart-shaped to rounded in different varieties.

TWIGS

Slightly zig-zag; hairy on new shoots, later
becoming smooth, shiny and red brown,
except for numerous whitish speckles; buds
brown, about 0.6 cm ($^1/4$ in.) long, faintly
downy, sometimes mildly resinous.

FLOWERS

Male in long drooping catkins that develop
from 2.5 cm-5.1 cm (1 in.-2 in.) catkins
formed the fall before and visible all winter;
the female much smaller and appearing with
the leaves; both on same twig; both elongat-
ing in April-May.

SEEDS

Tiny, two-winged nut borne by hundreds on
a drooping catkinlike cone; ripening in
autumn; shed during fall and winter.

BARK

Dark brown and thin at first, becoming many-
layered, chalky to creamy white (sometimes
with pinkish tinge); certain native varieties
also brownish; upper (younger) parts of
branches always brownish.

WOOD

Creamy white to pale brown; not as hard as
that of sugar maple or yellow birch, but
harder than that of red maple and aspen;
moderately strong; grain is faint; works easily
and takes a nice finish. Air-dry weight 641
kg/m^3 (40 lb./cu.ft.).

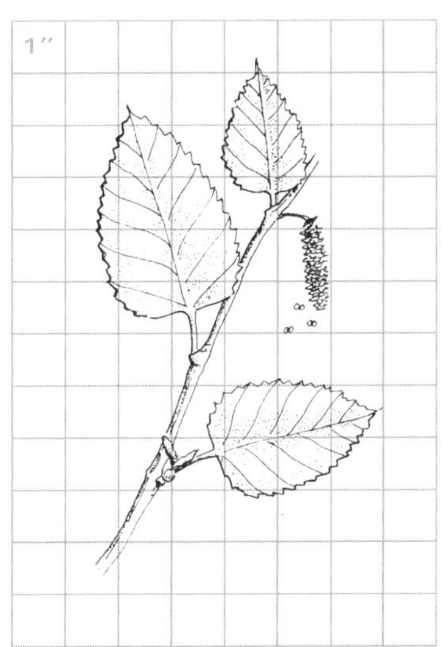

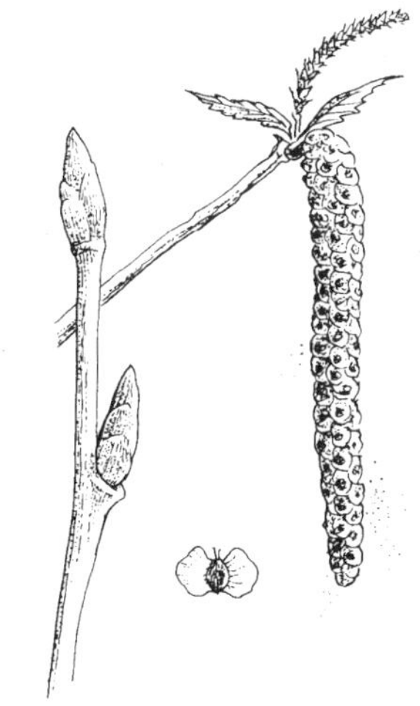

GREY BIRCH *Betula populifolia* Marsh.

Other common names: Wire Birch, White Birch

This small tree is often mistaken for young white birch, but the two species differ in several ways. In grey birch the dull chalky-white bark is tight and hard to peel, whereas the bark of white birch tends to be flaky, even on young trees. Also, the black triangles marking where limbs join the main stem are more pronounced in grey birch. Moreover, its leaves are on the average smaller, and much more drawn out at the tip. In winter, its slender wiry twigs are distinguished by their drooping habit, rough warty appearance, and slightly sticky buds.

Grey birch occurs from southern Ontario to the Maritimes and south to Delaware. Because of its small stature and its habit of quickly invading abandoned pastures, burns, and barrens, it is regarded by many as a weed tree. In this province it is most common in the western counties, being more or less replaced by white birch eastward.

Sometimes it serves as a useful nurse crop for young pine, but unless the grey birch saplings are cut early they will later crowd out the pine. Fuel wood, barrel hoops, and spool wood are its chief uses. Many birds eat the seeds.

INTRODUCED BIRCHES

The only foreign birch commonly seen is the European or weeping birch (*B. pendula* Roth) and its cut-leaf variety. The bark and leaves resemble those of our grey birch, although the bark is more flaky, and the leaf is more rounded at the base, with a less long-pointed tip. The cut-leaf variety has a V-notched leaf.

Another European import, white birch (*B. alba* L. or *B. pubescens* Ehrh.), may occur, but it has not been definitely reported. It resembles the native white birch but has smaller leaves and quite resinous buds.

IRONWOOD *Ostrya virginiana* (Mill.) K.Koch

Other common names: Hornbeam, Hophornbeam

Nova Scotia's hardest and heaviest native wood comes from this small member of the birch family. It is a slender tree with leaves much like those of yellow birch. The bark is light brown and scaly, and the twigs are tough and wiry without a wintergreen taste.

The seeds are greenish nutlets borne in clustered, bristly, bladderlike sacs on a slender stem. They develop from short greenish female catkins that appear in spring on the same twig with similar, pre-formed male catkins. A useful summer identification feature is the tiny stalked glands that usually appear on new twigs, on leaf stems, and on the underside of the leaf veins.

In winter, ironwood is best identified by its bark and twigs. The bark tends to shred off in narrow, scaly, curling strips. Often it shows a distinct spiralling pattern up and down the trunk. The twigs resemble those of grey birch in that they are a dark red brown, very slender, and wiry. They differ in that they are shiny and lack warty glands.

The tough, shock-resistant wood is whitish to pale brown and takes a good polish. It is very hard to nail. The air-dry weight is about 801 kg/m^3 (50 lb./cu.ft.).

Roland and Smith report that ironwood, although scattered from Annapolis County to Cape Breton, is rare except along intervales and on alluvial soils in the central part of the province. Ralph Johnson adds that it is found on well-drained soils in North Queens. The tree occurs throughout eastern North America.

Because of its scarcity and small size, ironwood is not much used except for firewood, tool handles, and sled-runners.

Grouse eat the winter buds.

SPECKLED ALDER *Alnus rugosa* (Du Roi) Spreng.

Other common names: Grey Alder

Of the three native alders, not to be confused with the elder (*Sambucus* spp.), which has a compounded leaf, speckled alder is the only one which reaches tree size. When it does, it is usually leaning, crooked, and much branched. Most people are familiar with its speckled grey bark and double-toothed, finely wrinkled leaves (bluish white or green below, depending on the variety).

Other useful identification features are its stalked, two-scaled buds borne on twigs with a three-cornered pith; its drooping, yellowish male catkins (formed the autumn before); and its oval, brown-black seed-cones, which turn woody and often remain on the tree all winter. Speckled alder occurs in dense thickets on low ground throughout the province.

Because alder roots bear nitrogen-rich nodules, drained alder flats can be quite fertile and suitable for raising leafy vegetables. It is said that the best way to clear an alder-bed is to fence it, let one or two pigs root about in it for a summer, and then remove the dead stems. Alder swamps in low-lying parts of softwood stands sometimes halt the progress of forest fires. Birds eat the small-winged nutlets, which resemble birch seeds.

BEECH *Fagus grandifolia* Ehrh.

A small to medium-sized branchy tree (in Nova Scotia) with smooth grey bark; long-pointed, straight-veined leaves; zig-zag twigs with long, sharp, tan buds; and paired edible nuts in a spiny bur.

Other common names: American Beech

American lumbermen have long been troubled by the slow but steady spread of a potent disease through their important stocks of beech. The disease is caused by the *Nectria* fungus aided by an insect called "beech scale." Both seem to have entered North America via Nova Scotia—the fungus about 1929 and the insect about 1890. Colonies of scale insects damage trees by piercing the bark and sucking sap. Later, wind-borne fungus spores infest the damaged tissues, which develop, spreading cankers that deform or kill the tree.

American beech ranges over all of eastern North America, except Newfoundland, the lower Mississippi, and southern Florida. In Nova Scotia it is common in the hardwood areas, being found on moist, well-drained slopes with maples and yellow birch. It also grows with red spruce, hemlock, and white pine. Though it tolerates heavy shade, pure beech stands sometimes clothe hilltops. Extreme cold damages this species, which is at its northern limit in Cape Breton.

Beech wood is used in woodenware, small furniture, and sometimes flooring. Mice, squirrels, bears, raccoons, and ruffed grouse eagerly seek the nuts. American settlers stuffed mattresses with the leaves, which stay springy longer than straw.

Beech bark was probably the first paper of our ancient European ancestors, and the words for "book" and "beech" are very similar in many North European languages (eg. Swedish *bok* can refer to either).

Introduced Beeches

European beech (*Fagus sylvatica* L.) is very similar to the native tree in bark, leaves, and twigs, though the leaves and twigs are smaller and the leaves less pointed. (The purple-leafed beech sometimes seen is a variety of this tree.) In Europe this beech is a large and important timber species. Its nuts are collected for hog-feed and cooking oils. Archaeologists have shown that the same species provided food for ancient cave-dwellers in the region.

LEAVES

Papery; dark blue green above, paler below
with straight side veins, each ending in a
tooth; smooth on both faces, except for
hair in the vein angles below; simple; alternate; often staying on the tree all winter.

TWIGS

Slender; zig-zag; shiny brown; buds alternate, pointing away from twig, nearly 2.5
cm (1 in.) long, with shiny brown scales.

FLOWERS

After the leaves; male in small yellow green
clusters; female in short spikes; both on
same tree.

SEEDS

Shiny, brown, sweet three-cornered nut;
borne in twos or threes inside a prickly
husk that splits open four ways upon
ripening around October.

BARK

A smooth grey blue, even in old age.

WOOD

Creamy to reddish brown; speckled in flat-
sawn wood with fine dark vertical dashes;
hard; heavy; strong (close to yellow birch
and sugar maple in these respects);
difficult to season, but takes a good polish.
Air-dry weight about 689 kg/m^3 (46
lb./cu.ft.).

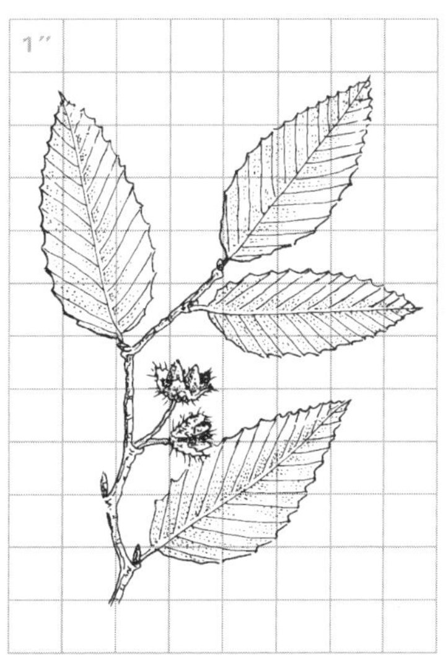

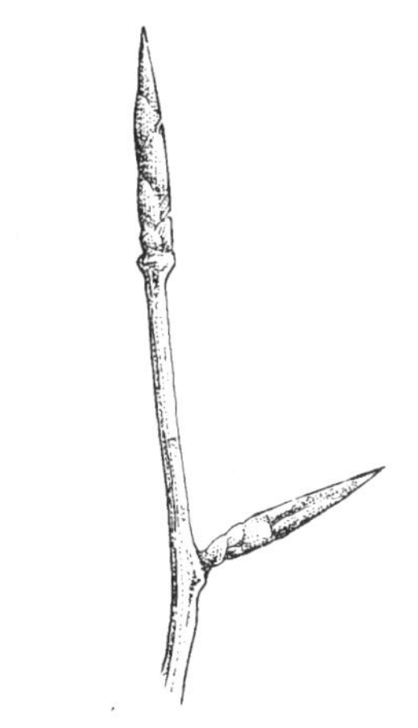

RED OAK   *Quercus rubra* L.

A fairly large, sturdy tree bearing dark green leaves with 7 to 11 bristle-tipped lobes, stout acorns, and twigs with a star-shaped core and a cluster of buds at the tip.

Other common names: Oak, Northern Red Oak

Red oak is found throughout Nova Scotia on light or well-drained soils. Johnson reports it as a common component of fire stands in western parts of the province, mixed with aspen, white birch, and grey birch. In some localities (Pleasant Bay, Cape North, and in parts of Queens County) there are pure stands. Roland and Smith say it was once common in the Annapolis Valley.

Outside the province this fast-growing, hardy oak ranges over most of eastern North America. It ranges farther north than any other species in the red oak group.

Because it prefers plenty of light, red oak is often found on sandy or rocky soils with light-loving species like aspen, white birch, or red maple. On such soils it does not grow large. On better sites it is usually seen with sugar maple, yellow birch, white ash, red spruce, and white and red pine. There it may reach 15 m-21 m (49 ft.-69 ft.) in height and 5.1 m-7.6 m (2 ft.-3 ft.) in diameter. It lives 200 to 300 years. Young trees sprout vigorously when the stem is killed by fire or cutting.

Furniture, flooring, and interior finish are its main uses. Unlike white oak, it cannot be used for leak-proof barrels because its open pores will not hold liquid. If you blow against the end surface of a short piece of red oak, the air passes right through.

In the open it develops a broad crown of stout branches, sometimes forking near the ground, making it an attractive ornamental. In autumn the foliage turns a deep crimson. The acorns are eaten by squirrels and deer.

The chief enemy of both forest and ornamental trees is the winter moth. Introduced to the Maritimes from Europe sometime before 1930, its caterpillars strip foliage. The forest tent caterpillar also attacks red oak.

Introduced Oaks

English Oak (*Quercus robur* L.) is sometimes seen along roads and streets, especially in the Annapolis-Halifax-Truro region. Its small round-lobed leaves and small oblong acorns are quite different from those of the native red oak, and its winter buds are hairless.

LEAVES

Dull dark green above, yellow green below; with tiny tufts of hair in angles of veins; the 7-11 lobes each tipped by a stiff bristle; often staying on tree during winter; simple; alternate.

TWIGS

Fairly stout; dark red to greenish brown; with alternate sharp-pointed usually fuzzy buds; larger tip buds, usually clustered; pith star-shaped in cross-section.

FLOWERS

Greenish; both sexes on the same tree; appearing before or with the leaves; the male a loose catkin; the female a cluster of tiny spikes.

SEEDS

Brown acorns of varying shapes mounted in many-scaled, cup-shaped to saucer-shaped base; needing two years to mature (small and flat the first year); bitter.

BARK

At first a smooth greenish brown; later dark brown to nearly black and broken into many wide, flat-topped ridges; finally developing narrow, corrugated ridges; inner bark orange or yellow.

WOOD

Pale reddish brown with rings or relatively large open pores marking the growth rings on the end-face; hard; heavy; strong (but less so than white oak). Air-dry weight about 689 kg/m^3 (42 lb./cu.ft.).

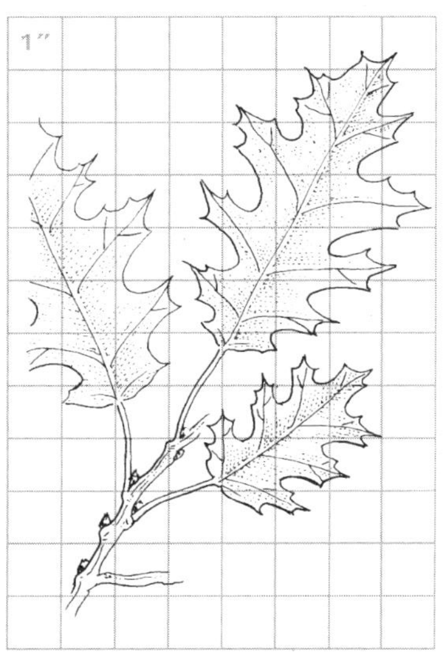

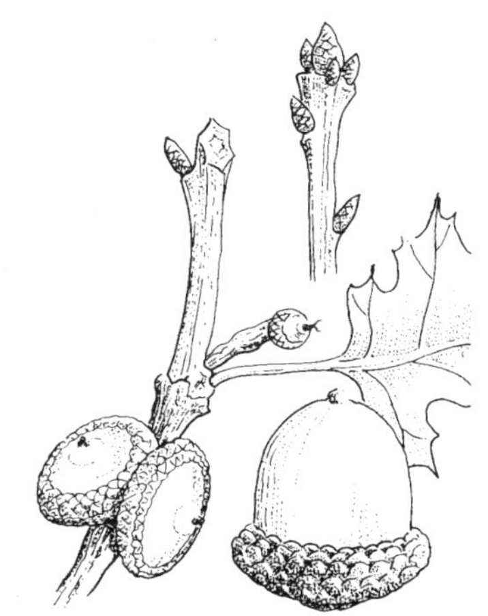

WHITE ELM *Ulmus americana* L.

A medium-sized to large, spreading (often vase-shaped) bottomland tree with variable, lopsided leaves, zig-zag twigs, and oval-winged seeds.

Other common names: American Elm, Elm

Because of its distinctive form and broad range (all of eastern North America), white elm is one of the best-known native trees. In Nova Scotia it occurs as a scattered tree along river flats, particularly through the central and northern counties, and in sheltered pockets on Cape Breton Island. In the open it forks near the ground and soon develops the familiar vase or umbrella shape. In the forest it produces a tall, straight trunk with a small crown.

Historically, white elm wood has been used for barrels to hold dry goods, pallets, fruit and vegetable containers. It has been a favourite urban ornamental.

Unfortunately, this species and its North American counterparts are vulnerable to Dutch Elm Disease (DED). The disease entered Canada in 1944 and has since spread to the prairies and the Atlantic coast. There are two types of DED found in Nova Scotia. In 1995 some counties remain free of it, but this will not last for long. Imports of elms—(*Ulmus*) and (*Zelcova*)—are not permitted. The domestic use and movement of elm wood is restricted.

The symptoms of DED are a sudden wilting and yellowing of the leaves on one or more limbs. Later, these leaves turn brown and shrivel. Leaf wilting is usually evident from late July to mid-August. Later the branch dies, and the disease spreads to adjacent parts of the tree. DED is carried from tree to tree by two species of bark beetles. Rarely, it will spread from an infected tree to an adjacent healthy tree by root grafts.

Sanitation is the best control for DED. A vigorous and sustained municipal tree health program will save the majority of urban elms.

Elms growing on flood plains are often flooded in spring. The seedlings can withstand this while dormant but will die if the water remains until the growing season. American elm can stand only moderate shade. It will reproduce vigorously from stump sprouts and root suckers. The winged seeds are carried up to a quarter-mile by wind, farther by water. Mice and birds eat many seeds.

LEAVES

Dark green and either smooth or sandpapery above, paler and usually hairy
below; lopsided at the base; often appearing two-ranked on twig; alternate; simple.

TWIGS

Slender; red brown; zig-zag; leaf-buds
pointed, slightly hairy, about 0.3 cm ($^1/8$
in.) long (flower buds rounded, larger);
branches becoming rough and corky with
age.

FLOWERS

Before the leaves; male and female combined in long-stemmed, loose clusters.

SEEDS

Small one-seeded samara with papery
wing fringed with fine hair; notched in the
form of a young bird's open beak; samara
falling early summer.

BARK

Grey; soon furrowed into fibrous, interlacing ridges; inner bark streaked with buff
corky patches; drooping branchlets present
along trunks of younger trees.

WOOD

Pale brownish, often with a fine wavy
grain; hard; heavy; extremely tough and
hard to split; bends and works well under
tools; and takes a good finish. Air-dry
weight about 673 kg/m^3 (42 lb./cu.ft.).

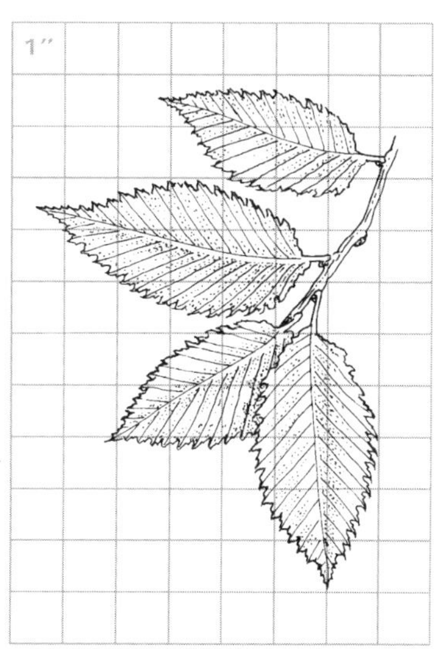

INTRODUCED ELMS

Three foreign elms are commonly seen: Scotch elm, English elm, and Siberian or "Chinese" elm. They can be separated by these differences:

SCOTCH ELM *Ulmus glabra* Huds.

Also called Wych elm, this species has wide, dark brown leaf buds and conspicuous rounded flower buds; coarse-toothed, sandpapery leaves that often look almost three-lobed near the tip; nearly circular hairless seed wings (about 2.54 cm or 1 in. across), and yellowish branches that stay smooth for many years.

ENGLISH ELM *U. procera* Salisb.

This large elm has a straight trunk with nearly horizontal branches; sandpapery lopsided leaves; small (about 1.3 cm or $^1/_2$ in.), somewhat heart-shaped, hairless samaras; moderately stout grey twigs with a warty, slightly fuzzy surface; and pairs of wedge-shaped scars near the buds.

SIBERIAN ELM *U. pumila* L.

A small spreading tree with small narrow leaves of a smooth, leathery texture, arranged in two distinct rows; hairy, zig-zag twigs; and small (0.9 cm or $^3/_8$ in.) samaras. Because of its resistance to Dutch Elm Disease, this Asian elm is becoming more popular as an ornamental than the European kinds. It may not be hardy enough for our climate, however. The foliage turns red to purple in autumn.

WITCHHAZEL *Hamamelis virginiana* L.

Other common names: Winter-bloom, Snapping-hazel

This strange looking little tree or large shrub has even stranger habits. It blooms in the fall, and shoots its seeds several metres with a loud snap. No other Canadian tree or shrub blooms in autumn.

Witchhazel is unmistakable in other ways. The alternate, simple leaves are lopsided with wavy edges instead of teeth—a combination not found in any other native shrub. The slender twigs are orange brown and more or less downy and bear hairy brown buds on short stalks. Often the top bud is curved. Witchhazel flowers, which are golden and appear in tangled clusters of three in September or October, have strap-shaped petals.

The shiny black seeds take a year to mature. They are found in a brown capsule about the size of a large pea. Splitting four ways, the capsule ejects its twin seeds with a snap, apparently in much the same way a youngster shoots an apple seed by pinching it between thumb and forefinger. Dried empty capsules remain on the tree over winter and help in identification. The bark is light brown, smooth or slightly scaly, and mottled.

Witchhazel is found over most of eastern North America. In southern parts it may grow to 7.6 cm (25 ft.) high. In Nova Scotia it is more often a large shrub with crooked spreading branches, growing in clumps on moist sites in rocky woods.

Roland reports it as common from Kings and Lunenburg counties to Colchester County but scattered westward and rarer eastward. Apparently it is absent from Cape Breton Island and Prince Edward Island.

Water diviners—people who claim to possess the ability to locate underground water—often choose a branch of this tree for the forked stick they use as an indicator.

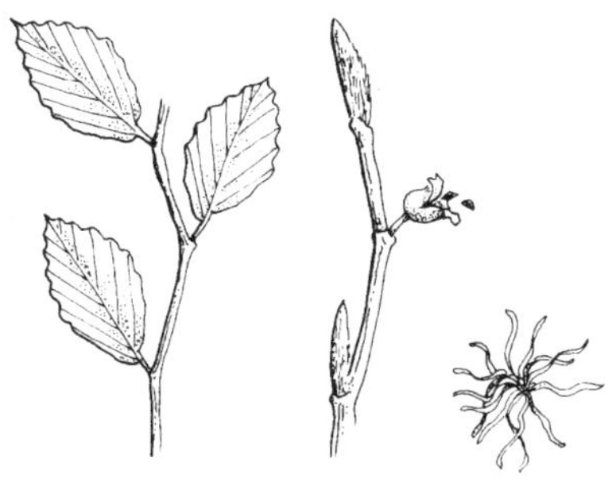

BLACK CHERRY *Prunus serotina Ehrh.*

A medium-sized tree having dark, shiny, fine-toothed leaves with a pair of glands on the stalk; reddish twigs with a bitter almond odour when broken; bearing dark red cherries in autumn.

Other common names: Wild Black Cherry, Wine Cherry

Black cherry, our largest native cherry, is found in southwestern and central Nova Scotia. In the central counties it is characteristic of rich or silty intervales, where it is mostly found mixed with other hardwoods. East of Antigonish it is rare because Nova Scotia marks the northern limit of the natural range of black cherry. It ranges westward to the Great Lakes, down to Arizona, across to Florida, and southward in pockets through the mountains of Mexico and Guatemala.

Black cherry yields one of the most prized furniture and cabinet woods. Sometimes it is cut locally for this purpose. A fast-growing tree, it prefers deep, rich soils. In Nova Scotia it normally reaches a height of 15 m-18 m (49 ft.-59 ft.) and a diameter of 2.5 cm 5.1 cm (1 ft.-2 ft.). Usually it lives for 150 to 200 years.

When covered with blossoms it makes an excellent ornamental. Unfortunately, in these latitudes late spring frosts can damage the flowers before they open, cause newly set fruit to drop, and kill newly germinated seedlings. Rabbits and deer account for much damage to seedlings and sprouts, and birds and squirrels consume large quantities of the fruit.

In common with other wild and cultivated cherry species, black cherry twigs and foliage contain a compound which releases cyanic acid when eaten. Domestic livestock can be poisoned by the foliage, while deer can eat it without ill effect. Symptoms of livestock poisoning include gasping and excitement. Wilted foliage is slightly more toxic than fresh foliage. Another product formed simultaneously with the odourless cyanide is oil of bitter almonds, which is the characteristic odour of crushed cherry twigs. The fruit is harmless.

Cherry cough remedies are made from the stewed bark of this species, so are tonic and sedative extracts. The fruit makes excellent jelly and wine.

LEAVES

Alternate; simple; glossy dark green above, paler below, with rusty brown hairs on the midrib near the base, and a pair of glands on the stalk; reddish twigs with a bitter almond odour; dark red cherries in autumn.

TWIGS

Slender; red brown (often with peeling greyish skin); top bud pointed and larger than side buds.

FLOWERS

White; 0.6 cm ($^1/4$ in.) wide; clustered on a drooping central stem; appearing when leaves half-grown.

BARK

Smooth; dark red brown at first, with long whitish lines across it; becoming rough and finely scaly with age (similar to spruce but darker).

WOOD

Pale brown to dark red brown; of average weight and hardness; has a pleasing grain, and takes a very fine polish; seasons easily; and takes glue well. Air-dry weight about 593 kg/m^3 (37 lb./cu.ft.).

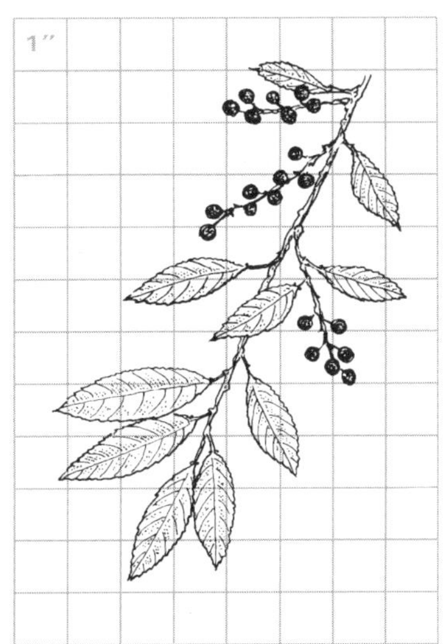

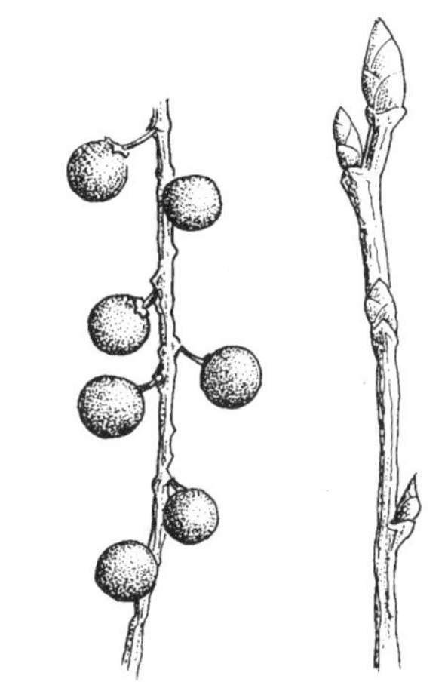

PIN CHERRY *Prunus pensylvanica* L.f.

A small tree having shiny lance-shaped leaves with two tiny glands on the stalk; smooth red-brown bark with orange dashes; red twigs with clustered end-buds; and scarlet cherries in autumn.

Other common names: Fire Cherry, Hay Cherry, Red Cherry, Bird Cherry

This tree is common, especially on recent burns and cutovers, on barrens, and in thickets along the edges of roads and fields. It prefers sandy soils and cannot grow in heavy shade. The seeds, being too heavy to blow on the wind, are spread by birds and animals. Deposits from birds also explain the prompt appearance of cherry species along fences and hedgerows. Allister Fraser cites evidence to indicate that these seeds may lie dormant for years, until fire cracks their hard shells.

"Pin cherry" refers to the arrangement of the fruit, which resembles red hat-pins radiating from a pin cushion. "Fire cherry" refers to its tendency to follow in the wake of fire. "Hay cherry" is used when the fruit ripens around haying time, and "bird cherry" recalls its dependence on birds for propagation. This species is found in the diet of at least 23 birds.

Mostly it is considered a forest weed because when it reaches 10.2 cm-15.2 cm (4 in.-6 in.) in diameter and 3 m-7.5 m (10 ft.-25 ft.) in height, it dies. It is valued as a pioneer species on newly cutover land, where its roots help hold bare soil in place, and its moderate shade protects the seedlings of more valuable species. The wood is sometimes used locally for fuel.

Some people transplant pin cherry to their lawns and gardens for its small stature, handsome bark, and crimson autumn foliage.

Like other native and cultivated cherries, the twigs and leaves of pin cherry contain cyanic acid and are poisonous. The fruit is harmless.

A fungus called "black knot" forms sooty, porous growths on the twigs and causes some damage. The best treatment is to remove the growths by cutting the twigs just below the infected parts.

LEAVES

Alternate; simple; thin; bright shiny green above, paler below; hairless; a pair of tiny glands near base of leaf.

TWIGS

Slender; smooth; shiny red brown; often with peeling greyish skin; buds tiny, rounded, with several clustered at twig tip; emitting almond odour when crushed.

FLOWERS

White; about 1.3 cm ($^1/2$ in.) wide, in four to five flowered umbrella-type clusters (not on a central stem as in black and choke cherries).

SEEDS

Bright red; in small clusters with the stems arising from one point (see choke and black cherry); edible; sour; with a rounded pit.

BARK

Thin; smooth; dark red brown with conspicuous raised orange lines across it when rubbed.

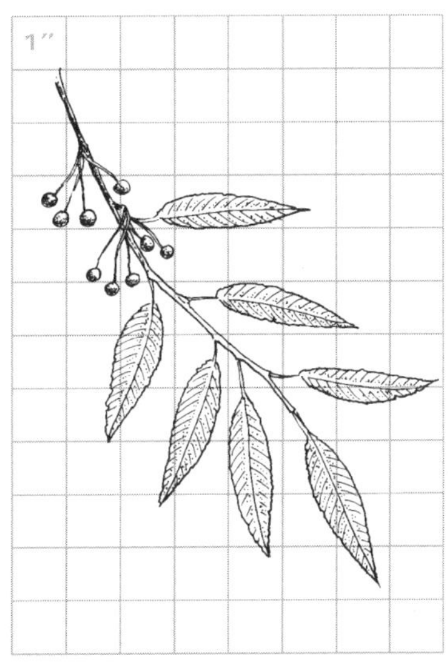

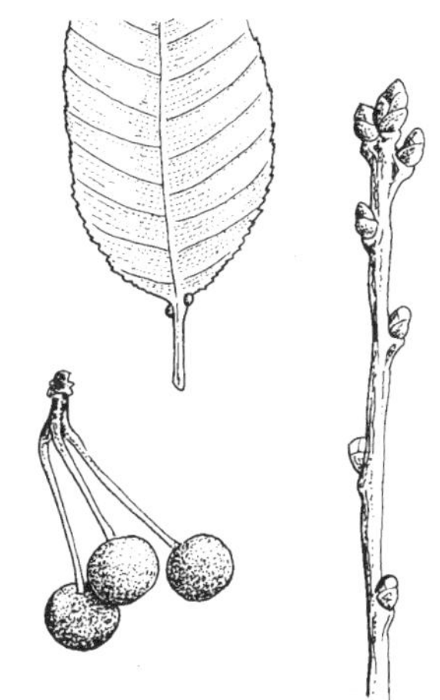

CHOKE CHERRY *Prunus virginiana* L.

A small, often crooked tree or shrub having broad dark green leaves that are widest above the middle, with a pair of glands on the stalk; brownish twigs with pointed buds and bitter-almond odour; and clusters of puckery red cherries in late summer.

Other common names: Wild Cherry, Red Choke Cherry

"It would be hard to find a more widespread and hardy shrub or small tree than choke cherry," writes Dr. W. M. Harlow in *Trees of Eastern and Central United States and Canada* (Dover, 1957). This smallest of our three native cherries is usually considered a weed. Choke cherry and its varieties thrive in every part of North America, except Mexico, Florida, and a few western states. Typically it will be found in sunny locations bordering meadows, streams, forest clearings, roads, fences, and rocky lake shores. In Nova Scotia it is more common in the northern parts, but occurs throughout.

As the name implies, its fruit tastes astringent or "puckery," but cooking removes this quality entirely.

The pectin-rich fruit is often used in preserves and jelly and makes an excellent red wine. After the first frost is the best time to pick it—but by that time birds have usually raided the trees.

The species is very frost-hardy. Prairie farmers often plant it for windbreaks. Its ability to root deeply and sucker freely makes it valuable for erosion control. Choke cherry also provides good cover and food for wildlife. Like black and pin cherry, it has poisonous twigs and foliage but harmless fruit.

LEAVES

Alternate; thin; dark green above, fine-toothed, paler and smooth below; wider above the middle; a pair of tiny glands just below the leaf.

TWIGS

Brown to grey brown, with pointed brown alternate buds covered by grey-edged scales; not clustered at the twig tip; with rank bitter-almond odour when crushed.

FLOWERS

White; after the leaves; bisexual; in a cone-like cluster along an upright stalk.

SEEDS

Yellow to dark red; juicy; edible but astringent (puckers the mouth); arranged around a drooping central stalk; having a rounded pit.

BARK

Thin; smooth; greyish without pronounced lines; roughened only on old trunks.

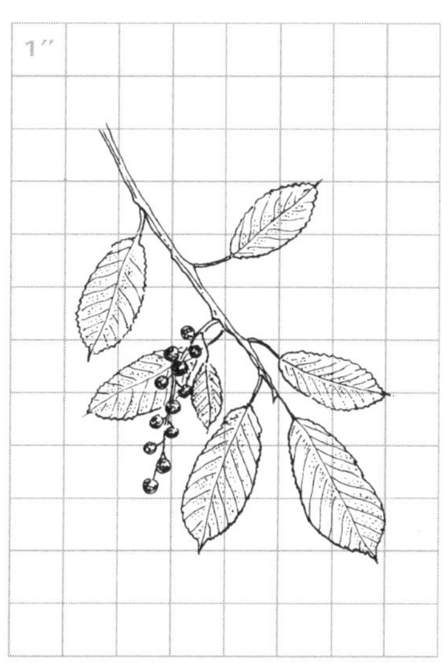

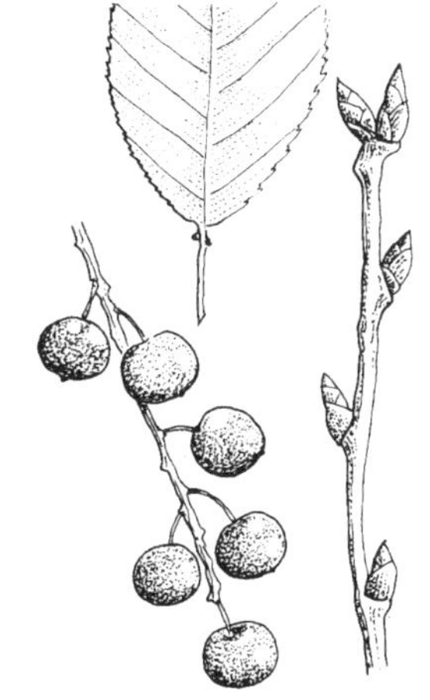

INTRODUCED CHERRY TREES

The genus *Prunus* includes plum, sloe, and peach, as well as cherry. Besides the three native cherry species, Nova Scotia has two or more introduced cherries, three introduced plums, and the imported sloe or blackthorn.

Information for identifying these and other introduced species may be found in any detailed handbook of northeastern flora such as Roland and Smith's *Flora of Nova Scotia.*

APPLE *Malus pumila* Mill.

Other common name: Wild Apple

Few people fail to recognize apple trees—winter or summer. Not many know that the tree we commonly call "wild apple," which is the parent of many of our cultivated strains, was originally introduced from Europe. (There are two native wild apples in Canada, but neither is native to this province.) Much planted in the early days, the cultivated strains have since escaped and gone back to the crabapple state which we call "wild apple."

ROSE FAMILY

This family of trees and shrubs deserves special mention because it is one of the most important to people. In Nova Scotia it accounts for over a dozen native and introduced trees and large shrubs. These are the various species of mountain-ash or rowan, cherry, hawthorn, serviceberry or shadbush, Canada plum, pear, and apple.

Other members of the rose family are the apricot, peach, and almond, along with such berries as strawberry, raspberry, loganberry, and blackberry. All have the common feature of five-petalled, usually showy flowers with combined male and female parts. Of the species described, only black cherry is valued for timber.

AMERICAN MOUNTAIN-ASH *Sorbus americana* Marsh

A small, much-branched tree bearing compound leaves made up of 11 to 17 fine-toothed, lance-shaped leaflets; flat-topped clusters of $^1/_4$-inch berries; and stout twigs with large gummy buds.

Other common names: Rowan-tree, Rowan-berry

This small, much-branched tree is not a true ash but a member of the rose family. In Nova Scotia it is common in open woods, on rocky hillsides, and along roads. Outside the province it ranges from Newfoundland to Manitoba and south to Tennessee. Its delicate leaves, showy white flowers, and scarlet "berries" add interest to the countryside, and it is often transplanted as an ornamental.

About a dozen kinds of birds eat the fruit, which often stays on the tree all winter. Birds tend to prefer them over the fruit of European mountain-ash, when both are available. Weather prophets claim that an abundance of mountain-ash fruit means a mild winter ahead. To us the fruit tastes bitter, but frost sweetens it slightly. They are said to be rich in iron and promote a good appetite. Well-aged "rowan-berry" or "dog-berry" wine is excellent. Deer and moose browse the twigs.

A similar native species is the showy or northern mountain-ash, commonly called dog-berry [*S. decora* (Sarg.) Schneid.]. Though not as common as the above species, it is scattered across the province, especially near shores.

The showy mountain-ash has larger fruits and flowers, and blunter, more boat-shaped leaflets with coarser teeth than the American mountain ash. The teeth seldom extend to the base of the leaflet as in American mountain-ash. However, these features are not always reliable because the two species appear to intergrade.

A commonly planted ornamental is European mountain-ash (*Sorbus aucuparia* L.), the true rowan of the Old World. From the Annapolis Valley to Amherst and Antigonish, it is common along roadsides. Although the flowers and fruit are similar to those of the two native species, the leaflets are fewer, smaller, rounded at both ends, and seldom toothed below the middle. In winter the grey twigs can be identified by their small, white, downy buds.

The leaf-eating mountain-ash sawfly is a pest on all three species.

LEAVES

Alternate; compound; 15.2 cm-25.4 cm
(6 in.-10 in.) long; composed of 11-17
leaflets borne in pairs on a fairly stout
team; leaflets narrow and finely saw-
toothed to, or nearly to, their bases,
tapering for about two-thirds their length
to a drawn-out, sharp point; bright green
above, paler and faintly hairy below.

TWIGS

Stout; smooth (sometimes slightly hairy);
red brown with whitish spots; buds large,
purple red, gummy; the tip bud 1.9 cm-
2.5 cm (^{3}⁄4 in.-1 in.)—about twice as big
as the side buds.

FLOWERS

June, after the leaves; in broad, flat-topped,
cream-white clusters.

SEEDS

August or September; scarlet; 0.6 cm (^{1}⁄4
in.); berrylike; in flat-topped, often drooping clusters that may persist over winter.

BARK

Thin; smooth; on young stems red brown,
turning grey on old stems.

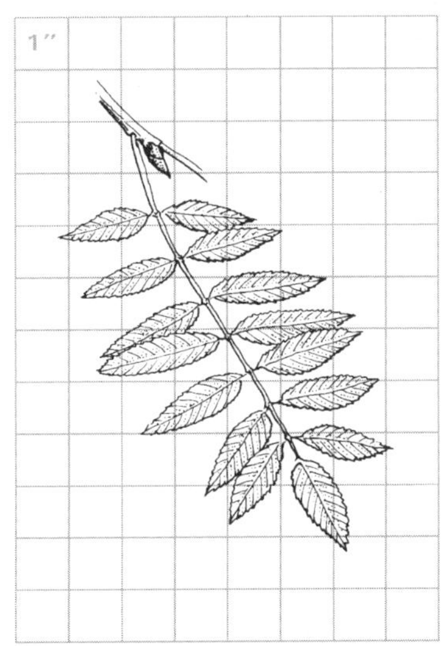

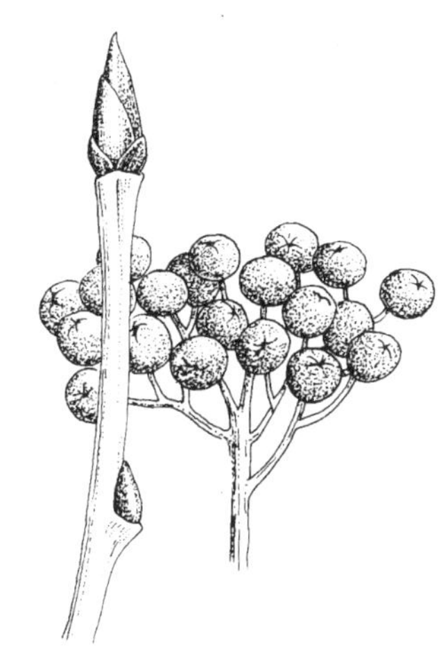

SHADBUSH *Amelanchier wiegandii* Nielsen, *A. laevis* Wieg, and others

Other common names: Wild Pear, Bilberry, Juneberry, Serviceberry

The shadbushes, of which the above two species commonly attain tree size
in Nova Scotia, are so named because they usually bloom when the shad are
running. Their narrow-petalled, white flowers make a striking display. Since
the several native *Amelanchier* species interbreed and the leaves on individual
specimens vary greatly, it is hard to identify them with certainty.

The leaves of shadbush are small, fine-toothed, thin, and without glands.
Those of *A. laevis* Wieg, are usually purplish when young. The winter twigs are
slender, bearing long-pointed buds covered by loose, hair-fringed scales. The
bark is smooth and greyish, turning scaly on old stems. Shadbush berries are
about 1.3 cm ($^1/_2$ in.) long, dark purplish, sweet and fairly juicy, and topped
by five withered flower parts. The leaves turn red to purple in autumn.
Clearings and cutovers are their common habitat.

AMERICAN HAWTHORN *Crataegus flabellata* (Spach) Koch var: *flabellata*

Other common names: Thorn, May-apple

Of about seven native hawthorns and two tree-sized species, this is the only one abundant enough to include here. It is a bushy tree-shrub with the trunk and larger branches often angled instead of rounded in cross-section, and twigs bearing clusters of small, soft, scarlet, applelike fruit containing several large seeds. The shiny red zig-zagging branchlets are armed with long sharp thorns—2.5 cm-5.1 cm (1 in.-2 in.) long—along their sides. The leaves are glossy above and coarsely double-toothed, and the flowers appear in white clusters. This tree is most common is western and central Nova Scotia, especially along rocky pastures, roadsides, and in woodlots.

An introduced hawthorn commonly seen is the one-seeded hawthorn (C. *monogyna* Jacq.), sometimes called English hawthorn. This tree-shrub differs in several ways from the native species. Its leaves are smaller, darker, and more deeply lobed; its winter twigs have the thorns on the tips of spur shoots; and its fruit is not multi-seeded. Both the native and introduced hawthorns commonly keep some of their fruit all winter. One-seeded hawthorn is most common in southern Nova Scotia, where it often escapes to roadsides.

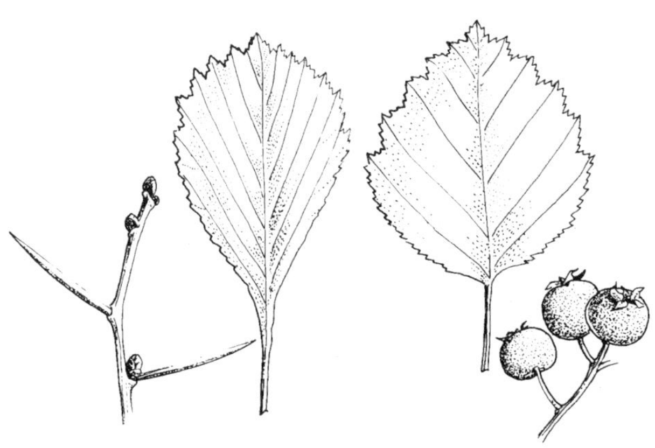

STAGHORN SUMAC *Rhus typhina* L.

Other common names: Sumac

Three things qualify this crooked little native tree or shrub for ornamental
use: distinctive shape, handsome foliage, and bird appeal.

In winter the stout, downy twigs and bare branches recall a spindly set of
antlers "in velvet"—hence the name. Dark brown hairs fuzz the twigs, and
the small scarlet "berries," which stay on the female trees all winter in large,
upright, cone-shaped clusters, are densely red-whiskered. The sexes are
separate.

In summer the out-sized compound leaves give sumac a flat-topped look.
These leaves are 0.3 cm-0.6 cm (1 ft.-2 ft.) long. They consist of 11 to 31
lance-shaped leaflets (up to 13 cm or 5 in. long) borne on a stout, hairy
stem. The colour is dull dark green above and silvery below. The only other
native tree with similar leaves is the American mountain-ash, but its leaf
stem is hairless and its leaflets are pale green below. Two other differences are
that sumac leaves exude a milky sap when broken, and its twigs have a soft
white pith.

In autumn, sumac puts on a spectacular display of flaming red foliage.
Through late summer and winter, scores of different bird species feed on the
fruit.

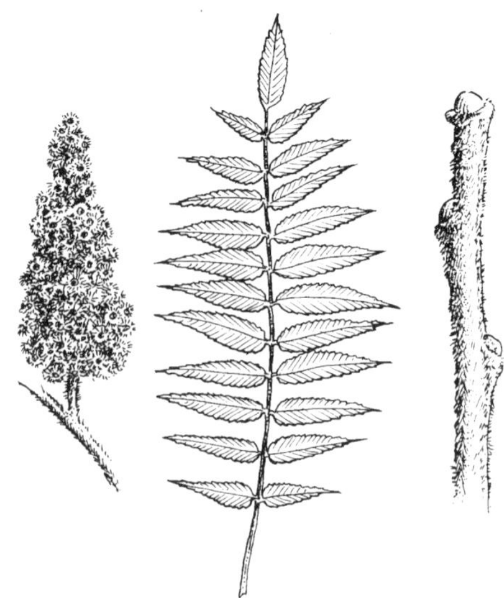

Rhus typhina L.

Staghorn sumac ranges from Cape Breton Island to Lake Huron, and south through the Appalachians to Georgia. In Nova Scotia it is most abundant in the southwestern counties, becoming rarer eastward. It grows best in dry and rocky soils on open hillsides, along roadsides, and in old fields.

Apart from its ornamental value, in the southern states this sumac was once a source of tannin. Also, the fruit was squeezed to make a refreshing drink called "Indian lemonade." Sucking the fruit cluster for its sour-apple flavour is said to be thirst-quenching, too. By punching out the pith from a twig, the settlers made a tube for sucking sap from sugar maples in spring.

Elsewhere the green-streaked orange wood is sometimes sawn into lumber for decorative finishing and for wooden novelties. Rabbits eat the winter shoots. Finally, E. T. Seton says that a black ink can be steeped from the leaves and fruit. Dr. Harlow adds that the ink can be improved and kept mould-free by adding a few drops of iron (ferric) salt.

SUGAR MAPLE *Acer saccharum* Marsh.

A medium-sized to large tree with short trunk, broad dense oval crown of wide five-lobed leaves with scalloped edges and few teeth; scaly grey bark; and shiny brown twigs with pointed buds.

Other common names: Rock Maple, Hard Maple

Sugar maple makes up only one-sixth of our hardwood forests, but it would be hard to do without. Its best growth occurs on rich, well-drained slopes in the Cape Breton, Cobequid and Musquodoboit uplands, and on the North and South Mountains of the Annapolis Valley. It is usually found mixed with one or more of yellow birch, beech, red spruce, hemlock, white pine, balsam fir, and occasionally beech and red oak. Sometimes pure stands occur, especially on the tops of rounded hills.

Sugar maple can stand a great deal of shade. It matures in 200 to 300 years and will grow to around 30 m (98 ft.) tall and 5.1 cm-7.6 cm (2 ft.-3 ft.) in diameter. Its native range is from Cape Breton to southeast Manitoba and south through the Missouri and Ohio watersheds to the end of the Appalachians in Georgia.

"What ash is to baseball," it has been said, "maple is to bowling." Sugar maple is probably unexcelled as a long-wearing, high-gloss flooring material such as that used in bowling alleys. Other uses include fine furniture, interior finish, vehicle stock, veneers and plywood, and sporting goods. Because of its excellent sound-enhancing qualities it is often used in musical instruments. From this tree also come fancy grain-patterns such as bird's eye and curly maple used in woodenware and furniture. Hard maple also makes an excellent firewood. A traditional industry still centres around the spring tapping of this species for its sap, to make maple sugar and syrup. It takes about 182 L (40 gal.) of sap to make 4.5 L (1 gal.) of syrup. Early settlers burned hard maple to obtain the potash needed to make soap.

The Bruce spanworm does some damage, as does a leaf-browning disease called anthracnose. Since the 1970s, widespread mortality of unknown origin has occurred; evidence points to acid rain and other pollutants.

LEAVES

Thin; with three to five lobes separated by rounded "coves"; teeth few; dark green above, paler below; turning wine, scarlet, orange, or yellow in autumn; opposite; simple.

TWIGS

Slender; shiny; reddish brown with whitish dots; buds opposite; sharp-pointed; leaf scars V-shaped.

FLOWERS

Yellowish clusters in May, with the leaves; some trees bearing only male, others with both male and male-female blossoms.

SEEDS

Clustered pairs (called "keys" or samaras) of red brown; winged seeds; ripening and falling in autumn.

BARK

Grey and nearly smooth on young stems; later splitting into deep vertical ridges that look like ploughed furrows.

WOOD

Pale brown; hard; heavy; very strong (tougher than white oak); easily finished to a fine, highly-polished surface with a pleasing grain in flat-sawn stock; of high shrinkage; difficult to nail; slow to absorb preservatives unless pierced first. Air-dry weight about 753 kg/m^3 (47 lb./cu.ft.).

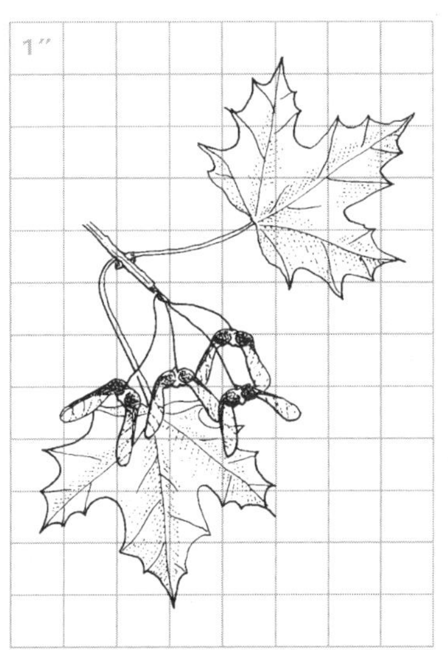

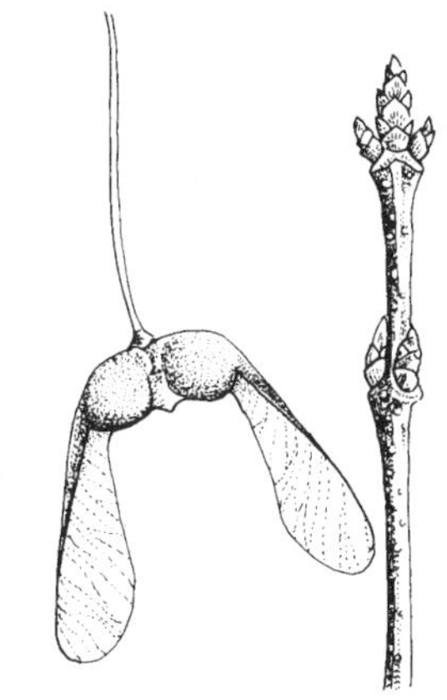

RED MAPLE *Acer rubrum L.*

A small to medium-sized, much-branched tree with grey scaly bark and upturned branches; bearing orange flowers in spring; red lobed leaves in spring and fall; red seeds, and dark red winter twigs.

Other common names: Soft Maple, Swamp Maple, White Maple

It is the leaf of this maple that has long been Canada's emblem, although that of sugar maple is sometimes seen in designs. The Canadian flag shows a symbolic leaf combining the features of various maples.

Actually, red maple is not found west of southwest Manitoba. It ranges south to Texas, east to Florida, and north to Newfoundland.

In Nova Scotia it is the most abundant hardwood, comprising over one-third of the total hardwood volume. It grows almost anywhere, from swamps to dry and rocky uplands. Because it often invades recent cutovers or burnt land, red maple is on the increase.

The wood is used for the same purposes as sugar maple, and, except where strength, hardness, or large size are critical factors, it is generally sold with sugar maple. Red maple is also popular as an ornamental. But the branches are prone to breakage in sleet storms, and rot sets in rapidly where scars are not cleaned and painted. Its scarlet autumn display is unexcelled among native species.

According to one botanist, a permanent black dye can be made by adding aluminum salts to a hot-water extract of the bark. But more useful is the syrup that this species yields in the spring. Although the tree gives less than its larger cousin, the sugar maple, early settlers tapped both maples when sugar was scarce. Deer and moose browse on the winter twigs.

LEAVES

Having three to five lobes with V-shaped notches and coarse sawteeth; green above, silvery green below; simple; opposite.

TWIGS

Slender; dark shiny red with whitish dots; buds opposite, rounded, dark wine with light-edged scales.

FLOWERS

Orange or yellow; appearing before leaves from conspicuous, clustered oval buds on twig tips; single trees may be male, female, or male-female.

SEEDS

Clustered pairs of red to reddish brown, winged seeds; ripening and falling in early summer.

BARK

At first smooth, light grey or reddish brown; later dark grey, brown with long narrow platy scales.

WOOD

Moderately hard; not strong; similar to sugar maple wood but with a greyish cast. Air-dry weight about 609 kg/m^3 (38 lb./cu.ft.).

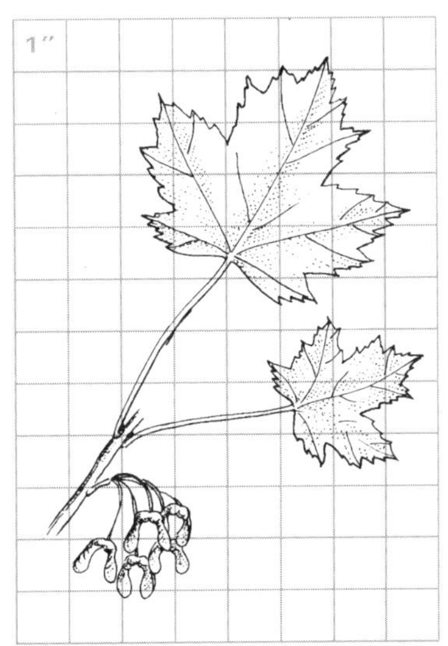

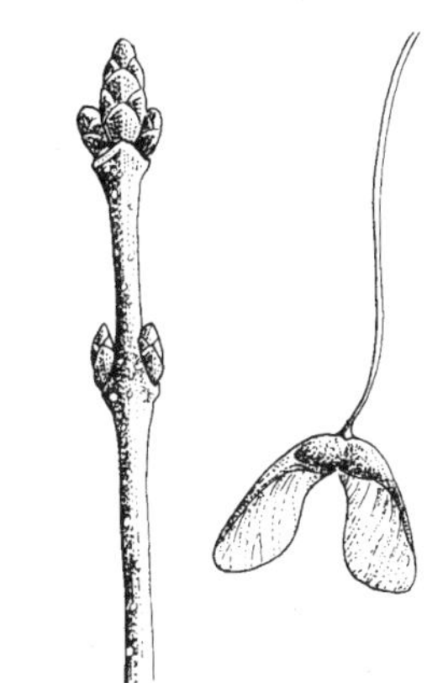

MOUNTAIN MAPLE *A. spicatum* Lam.

Other common names: White Maple, Whitewood, Dwarf Maple

This smallest of eastern maples is unusual in that its yellow-green flowers appear in an erect conical spike (hence the Latin *spicatum*), with the male blossoms around the top and the female around the bottom. The female flowers develop into small pairs of samaras which, as they ripen, change from scarlet or yellow to brown. They fall in September.

Mountain maple is also known by its three-lobed (sometimes five-lobed), coarsely toothed leaves that have wrinkled vein patterns on the upper surface and are slightly hairy and paler below.

In winter the species is known by its slender and brittle red twigs and their stalked opposite buds. Another useful identification feature at this season is the presence of a grey down on the last inch or so of the twigs. The thin bark is greenish and smooth when young, becoming red brown or grey brown and furrowed at maturity.

Mountain maple grows in shady spots on moist rocky slopes and flats, and along streams and moist roadsides, rarely reaching a height of 7.6 m (26 ft.). It ranges from Newfoundland to Saskatchewan and south to North Carolina. On the highlands of northern Cape Breton it is especially abundant. Often it is found with striped maple. Deer and moose browse them both at all seasons. Ruffed grouse are fond of the winter buds. Though not big enough for any commercial or domestic use, the species is important in preventing erosion of steep banks and slopes.

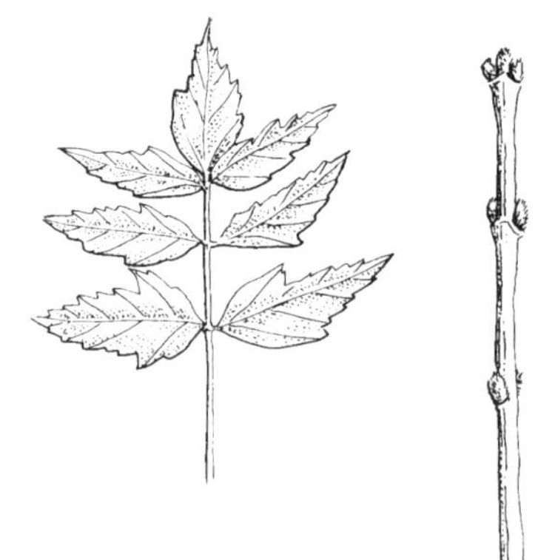

STRIPED MAPLE *A. pensylvanicum* L.

Other common names: Moosewood, Moose Maple

Striped maple gets its common name from the conspicuous vertical white stripes on its smooth greenish
to brownish bark. Another distinctive feature of this
small, much-branched tree-shrub is its large, pale,
three-lobed leaf featuring drawn-out tips. The yellow
flowers, unlike those of mountain maple, are arranged
in long drooping clusters. Usually the male and female
flowers are on different trees. The samaras are greenish, and the seed cavity is pitted on one side.

Like mountain maple, moosewood is found
throughout the province, though not as abundantly. It prefers cool, rich,
shaded slopes, especially with yellow birch, beech, other maples, red spruce,
and hemlock. As food for wildlife and as a soil stabilizer, it serves the same
purposes as mountain maple.

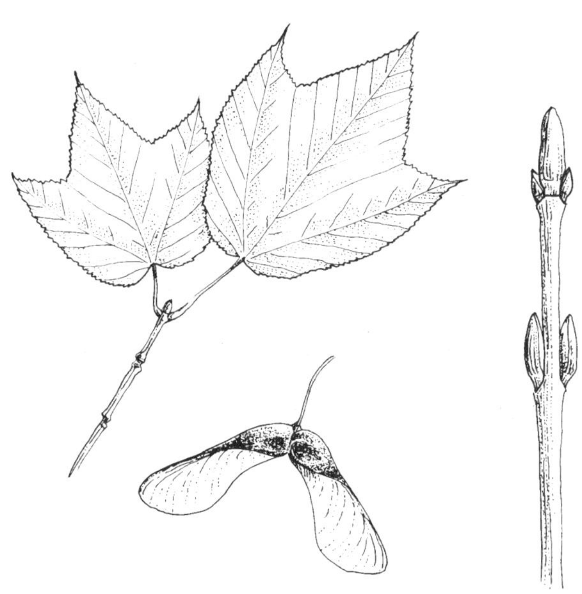

INTRODUCED MAPLES

At least four introduced maples are seen in the province. Two are North American species and two are European species. The two North American imports are silver maple and Manitoba maple. The two exotics, from Europe and Asia, are Norway maple and sycamore maple. Other Eurasian species may be present too.

SILVER MAPLE   *A. saccharinum* L.

A medium-sized to large tree with five-lobed, deeply U-notched opposite leaves that are bright, shiny green above and silvery white beneath; shiny red to orange-brown twigs that give off a disagreeable odour when crushed; and smooth to furrowed greyish bark. A handsome ornamental, but prone to storm breakage. The range is from southwestern New Brunswick through southern Ontario and most of the eastern United States.

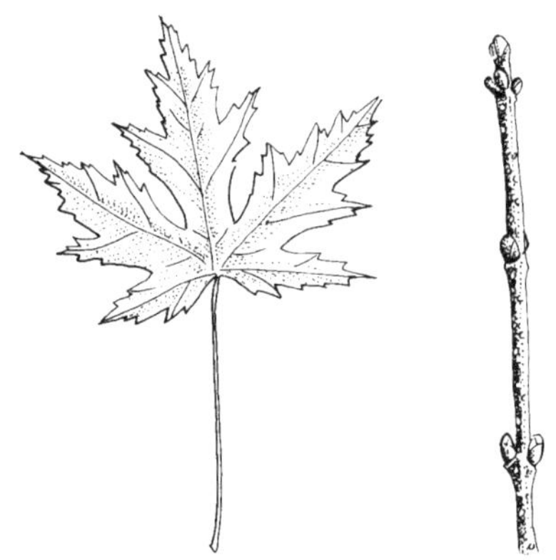

Sometimes silver poplar is called "silver maple" because its leaves look similar, especially when seen from a distance on a windy day.

MANITOBA MAPLE   *A. negundo* L.

This much-branched, smallish tree is the only Canadian maple with a compound leaf. The resemblance of this leaf to that of elder (*Sambucus* spp.), and the fact that elsewhere its wood is used for making boxes, accounts for the alternate name box-elder. The unique opposite leaves often have lobed lower leaflets. The smooth twigs are usually greenish (often with a whitish coating) and have downy, bluish-white buds. The range includes the prairie provinces and most of the United States.

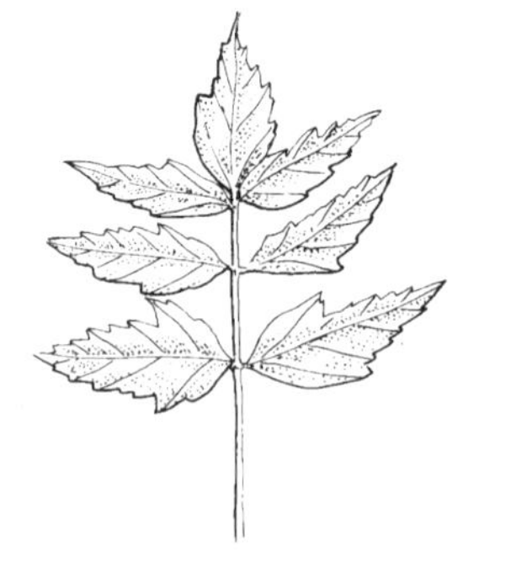

NORWAY MAPLE *A. platanoides* L.

This tree might be thought of as the European counterpart of our sugar maple. Both are similar in general appearance, and both are valuable timber species. But in North America, we value Norway maple for its ornamental excellence. As a shade tree it is not only handsome, but its resistance to smoke, dirt, fumes, insects, and disease makes it ideal for street planting. In Nova Scotia it is very popular.

Distinguishing features include the thin, long-stemmed leaf with usually seven lobes instead of five; the milky sap exuded when a leaf is crushed; and the fact that the two halves of the winged fruit extend almost in a straight line. (Eastern maples have their samaras joined at angles of not much over 90°.) The winter twigs are stout, with a large red terminal bud and close-pressed red side buds.

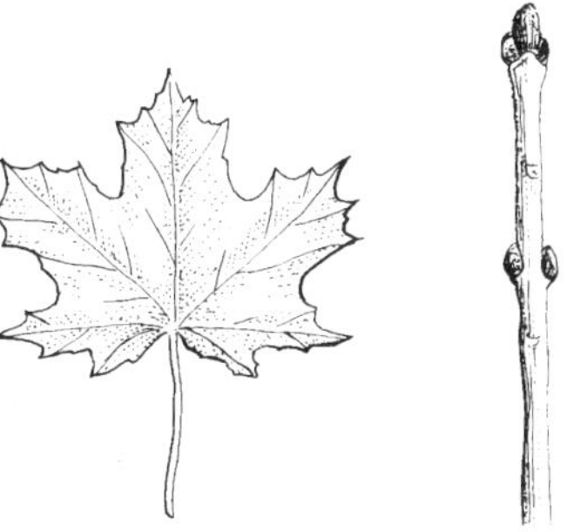

SYCAMORE MAPLE *A. pseudoplatanus* L.

Also called planetree maple, this large native of Europe and Asia may occasionally be seen along our streets. It is not as hardy as Norway maple. Distinguishing features are the coarsely round-toothed, five-lobed leaves, dark green with sunken vein lines on the upper surface and pale green below; the stout twigs with divergent green side buds and large green tip bud; and the 7.6 cm-17.78 cm (3 in.-7 in.) hanging clusters of yellow-green flowers.

WHITE ASH *Fraxinus americana* L.

A multiple-leafed tree of medium to large size with stalked, hairless leaflets; finely furrowed ash-grey bark; winged paddle-shaped seeds; and stout greenish winter twigs, with dark opposite buds and prominent V-notched leaf scars.

Other common names: Ash, American Ash

Of the four native ashes in Canada and the three in Nova Scotia, white ash has the finest wood. To rephrase the statement made about sugar maple, "ash is to baseball what maple is to bowling." Since ash bends and absorbs shock without breaking, it is frequently used for baseball bats and hockey sticks. It is ideal for long-handled tools, and for bentwood construction in furniture, wagons, snowshoe and tennis-racquet frames, boatbuilding, barrels, and trunks.

This ash ranges from Nova Scotia to Minnesota and south to the Gulf States. Most common in central Nova Scotia, this species prefers deep, moist soils on lower slopes and along streams and is always found mixed with other species such as beech, birch, maple, and hemlock. Its handsome bark and foliage make it a fine ornamental.

The winged seeds may travel up to 137 m (449 ft.) from the parent female trees. They germinate best on moist, fertile soil in sunny locations without plant competition.

Early growth is rapid. Open-growth saplings may reach a height of 1.5 m-1.8 m (5 ft.-6 ft.) in three to five years, and sprouts from young trees may grow 1.5 m (5 ft.) in their first year. In this province white ash grows to 18 m (59 ft.) or taller and 0.6 m-0.9 m (2 ft.-3 ft.) in diameter.

Shaded side branches soon drop off, leaving a clean bole. This species can withstand shade in youth but has less tolerance as it matures. White ash develops a straight trunk with few branches below the main crown. In the open, however, old trees may spread their crowns as widely as any elm.

Seeds are eaten by purple finch, pine grosbeak, wood duck, and other birds. The shoots are browsed by beaver and deer, and cattle relish them. Porcupines like the bark. Among insect enemies, the forest tent caterpillar does some damage.

LEAVES

Compound; opposite (ash and maple are
our only native trees with opposite buds
and leaves); 20.3 cm-30.48 cm (8 in.-12
in.) long; made up of five to nine smooth,
sparsely toothed leaflets; dark green above,
paler below.

TWIGS

Stout; smooth; lustrous, with a jointed
appearance; grey green to brown green,
bearing dark brown buds above conspicuous, V-notched (think of the double-V in
W) leaf scars (black ash leaf scars are flat to
slightly U-shaped on top).

BARK

Smooth, sometimes with an orange cast on
young stems; otherwise ashy grey; developing a fine diamond-shaped network of
interlacing, flat-topped ridges.

FLOWERS

With or before the leaves; male and female
on different trees; borne in stout clusters
near the branch tips.

SEEDS

With a thin wing at one end (see black and
red ash); in clusters that often stay on the
tree into winter, rustling in the wind.

WOOD

Heavy; hard; very tough; pale brown with
lines of open pores along the growth
rings, that are usually wider than in black
ash. Air-dry weight about 705 kg/m^3 (44
lb./cu.ft.).

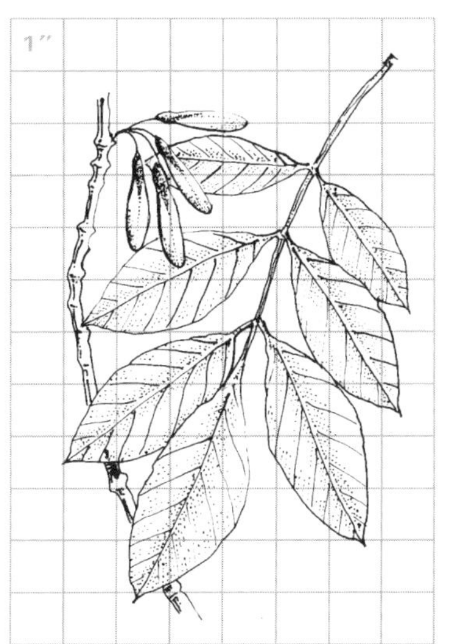

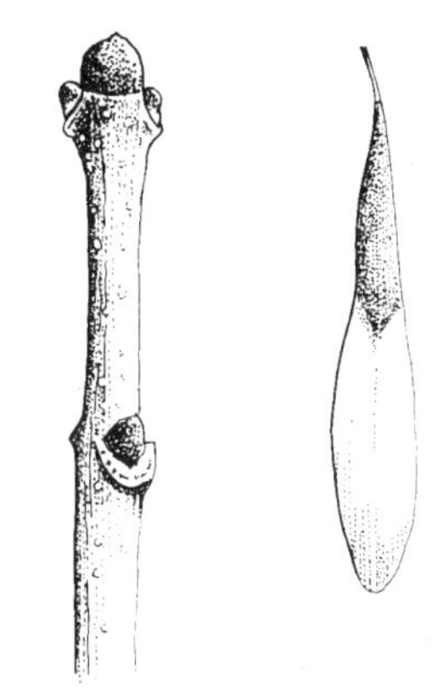

BLACK ASH *Fraxinus nigra* Marsh.

A small to medium-sized slender tree of wet ground; bearing compound leaves with narrow, stalkless leaflets; grey twigs with nearly black buds above unnotched leaf scars; and winged paddle-shaped seeds with the wing enclosing the seed.

Other common names: Swamp Ash, Water Ash, Basket Ash, Brown Ash

Black ash has been a staple in basket-making. Barked logs were soaked in water then pounded with wooden clubs until flat, thin slats could be peeled off. These slats were split and fashioned into strong baskets.

Two features make this ash popular for basketry. One is that its annual rings have conspicuous lines of open springwood vessels or pores. On a log face these openings appear as concentric circles. They weaken the wood crossways, causing the yearly layers to separate like onion layers when softened and pounded. Secondly, black ash is a slow-growing tree, meaning the lines of weakness occur close together, which is ideal for peeling off thin slats.

Modern veneer-making employs a similar process, except that a fixed blade slices from the spinning log a uniform sheet of wood, regardless of the position of annual rings.

Black ash is a tree of open wet places and it is intolerant of shade. It grows in openings along the margins of swamps and streams, or near springs. Seeds often lie dormant for a year or more before germinating.

Common associates are red maple, speckled alder, willow, fir, or cedar. It reaches heights of 12 m-15 m (40 ft.-50 ft.) and diameters up to about 0.3 m (1 ft.). The root system is very shallow. The trunk is seldom as straight as that of white ash.

In Nova Scotia, black ash is most common from Digby and central Lunenburg counties to northern Cape Breton; elsewhere it is scattered or rare.

Because of its scarcity, the wood has never been commercially important in Nova Scotia. Elsewhere it is used, in the better grades, for the same purpose as white ash lumber.

LEAVES

Opposite; 25.4 cm-40.6 cm (10 in.-16 in.) long; compound; composed of 7-11 stemless narrow leaflets with fine teeth and tufts of hair along midvein below; dark green above, paler beneath.

TWIGS

Stout; smooth grey; somewhat flattened at the joints; opposite, nearly black buds, the tip bud conical; leaf scars level to slightly concave across the top, and marked by a curved line of dots (about 16).

FLOWERS

September, in oblong samaras with wing completely enclosing the seed; shed in late autumn or early winter.

BARK

Smooth and grey; becoming slightly roughened to shallow-furrowed (but without diamond-shaped pattern).

WOOD

Whitish to dark brown, with close growth rings marked by rings of open pores; moderately heavy and hard; not nearly so strong as white ash, but with a more pronounced grain; takes a good finish. Air-dry weight about 561 kg/m^3 (35 lb./cu.ft.).

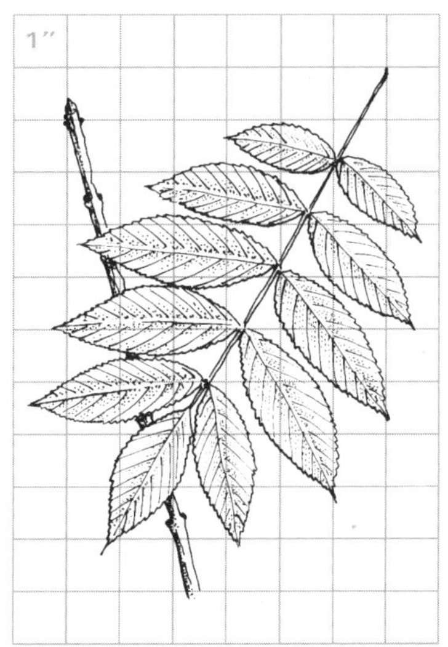

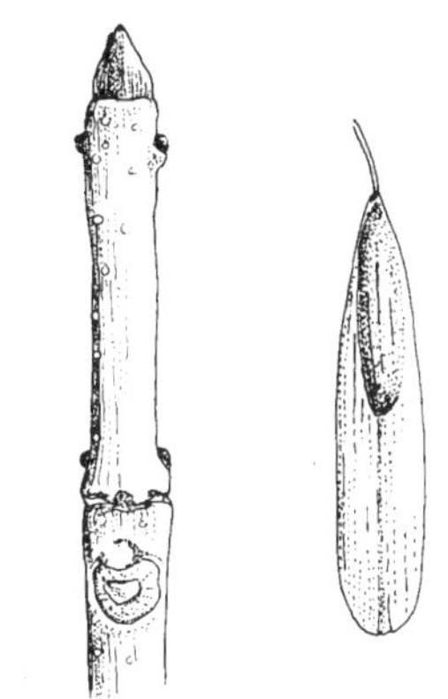

RELATED AND INTRODUCED ASH

Northern red ash (*F. pennylvanica* Marsh. var. *austini* Fern.) is rare in Nova Scotia but is sometimes seen with black or white ash. It resembles the latter in having broad, stalked leaflets, but its leaflets are pale yellow green and have hairy stalks and abundant teeth. Also, a velvety hair covers the twigs, buds, and main leaf-stalks, and the mature bark is a red-tinged brown.

OTHER INTRODUCED SPECIES

In this book, introduced species have thus far been described along with their native relatives. However, certain commonly seen exotic species lack any close local relatives. Brief descriptions of some of these exotics follow.

Linden *Tilia europaea* L.

Other common names: Basswood, European Linden, Lime

This large tree has a dense crown of broadly heart-shaped, long-stemmed, 5.1 cm-10.2 cm (2 in.-4 in.) leaves growing in two rows along the twig. The twigs are zig-zagged and brownish, with distinctive shiny red to pale green buds covered by only two or three scales, of a texture and colour like apple skin. The leaves and buds are lopsided in appearance.

An odd feature of this tree is that its small, rounded grey fruits are borne in clusters on a stalk attached along half its length to a strap-shaped papery blade. The blade serves as a wing or parachute when the fruits drop in late summer.

Apart from the value of lindens as ornamentals, bee-keepers sometimes plant them near hives because the late-blooming, pale yellow flowers provide a good source of honey after clover goes to seed.

This tree has a very similar North American counterpart, namely American basswood (*T. americana* L.). Basswood ranges from Lake Winnipeg to Tennessee and north to the Saint John River Valley of New Brunswick. Doubtless it would thrive in Nova Scotia. Its leaves are nearly twice as large as those of the European species.

The linden family, which is mainly tropical, includes many valuable timber species. Rope was once made from the tough and fibrous inner bark or bast (hence, "basswood"). Bast fibres from several tropic herbs of the linden family yield jute for burlap bags and cordage.

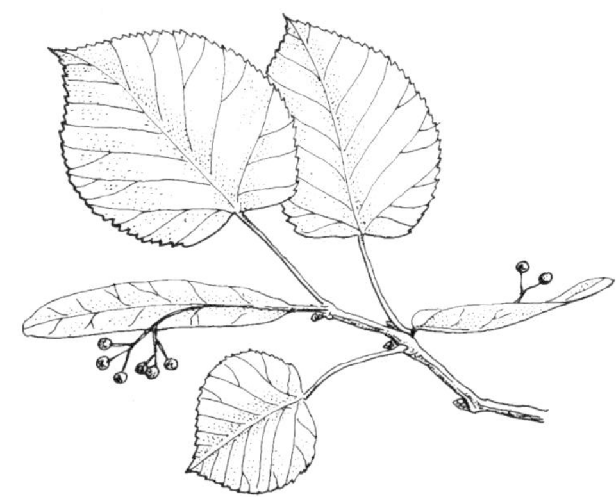

Horse-Chestnut *Aesculus hippocastanum* L.

Seven leaflets arranged like the fingers of a hand are the best summer guide
to this medium-sized to large ornamental from the Balkan peninsula.
Another distinctive feature, at least in June, is its showy upright cone of
white blossoms (pinkish to red in one variety). In winter the very stout
twigs are a sure guide. They have pronounced horseshoe-shaped leaf scars
(with five dots each for nails), and large, gummy, blackish buds.

The shiny brownish-black nuts of this shade tree grow encased in a spiny
bur as big as a golf ball. They are not edible like real chestnuts.

One writer claims that the meat of horse-chestnuts, when ground to a
flour, will make a book paste that repels the ticks which sometimes destroy
book-bindings in libraries. The fresh seeds are thought to be poisonous.

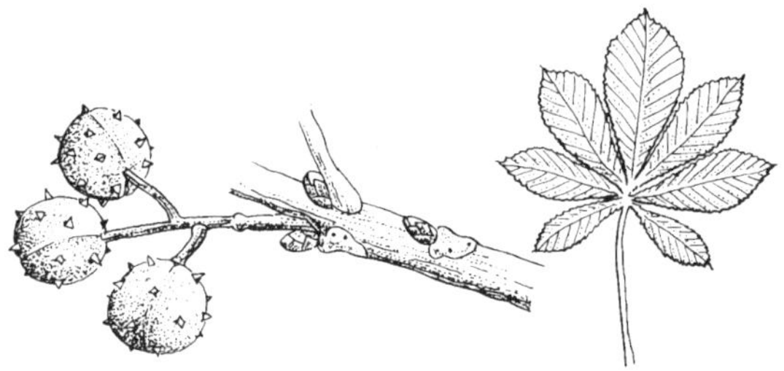

Locusts

Two species of locust are frequently seen in the province, especially in the
western counties, where they have been commonly planted as ornamentals.
They are black locust (*Robina psuedoacacia* L.), and clammy locust (*R. viscosa*
Vent.). A third, bristly locust (*R. hispida* L.), is only found south of Wolfville,
according to Roland and Smith.

Black locust is a large ornamental with fernlike, blue-green compound
leaves, paired spines, fragrant blossoms, and beanlike pods. It is native to the
Appalachian and Ozark Mountains. The sharp 0.6 cm ($^1/_4$ in.) spines occur
just above where the leaf stalk joins the twig. Locust twigs are red brown,
somewhat zig-zag, and angled in cross-section. When old, the tree has
deeply-furrowed, dark brown bark, looking almost as if rough old rope had
been braided and interlaced up and down the trunk.

Where black locust is more plentiful, its durable wood is used for railway ties, fence posts, and insulator pins. In Nova Scotia, its very fragrant white "sweet-pea" flowers and handsome foliage made this species one of our most popular ornamentals in years past.

Clammy locust is a small introduced relative that is often seen in clumps or thickets in the Annapolis Valley. Its leaves are similar to those of black locust, but the twigs are sticky and the flowers rose purple.

Honey-locust (*Gleditsia triacanthos* L.), a relative of the true locusts, is occasionally seen. Also imported from the south-central United States, this large ornamental has leaves resembling those of black locust, except that they are usually doubly compound (i.e., arranged as if a number of compound leaves were spaced along one stem), and the leaflets are smaller. Other differences are its large usually three-branched thorns (hence the Latin *triacanthos*) and its huge—up to 45.7 cm (18 in.) long—shiny seed pods. The flowers are small and plain. Nurseries usually sell thornless, seedless varieties of this hardy species.

The locusts and honey-locusts are members of the bean or pea family.

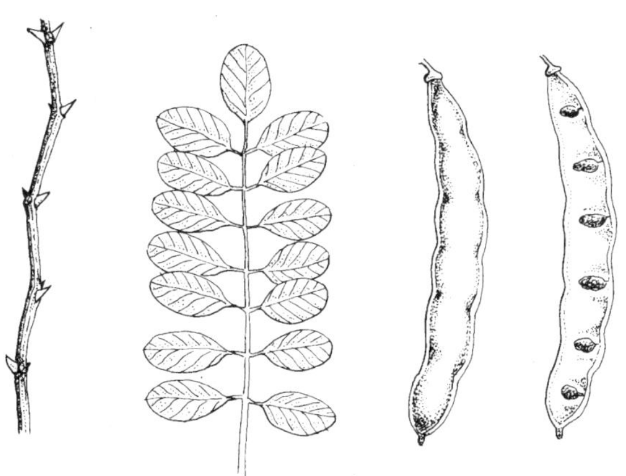

REFERENCES

Benson, D. A. and Roland, A. E.; **Summer Key to the Woody Plants of Nova Scotia** (Bull. No. 16), N.S. Department of Lands & Forests, Halifax, 1955.

Bulmer, R. M. and Hawboldt, L. S.; **The Forest Resources of Nova Scotia**, N.S. Department of Lands & Forests, Halifax, 1958.

Canadian Forestry Service; **Canadian Woods: Their Properties and Uses**, Eds. E. J. Mullins, T. S. McKnight; Canadian Government Publishing Centre, Ottawa, 1981.

Davidson, A. and Prentice, R. M.; **Forest Insects and Diseases of North America**, Queen's Printer, Ottawa, 1967.

Donly, J. F.; **Identification of Nova Scotia Woody Plants in Winter** (Bull. No. 19), N.S. Department of Lands & Forests, Halifax, 1960.

Harlow, W. M.; **Trees of the Eastern and Central United States and Canada**, Dover Publications, Inc., New York, 1957.

Harlow, W. M., Harrar, E. S., and F. M. White. **Textbook of Dendrology**, McGraw-Hill Book Company, Inc., Toronto, 6th Ed., 1979.

Hosie, R. C.; **Native Trees of Canada**, Fitzhenry & Whiteside, Toronto, 1979.

Johnson, H.; **The International Book of Trees**, Simon and Schuster, New York, 1973.

Keeler, H. L.; **Our Northern Shrubs and How to Identify Them**, Dover Publications, Inc., New York, 1969.

Kingsbury, J. M.; **Common Poisonous Plants**, New York State College of Agriculture, Ithaca, New York, 1965.

Muenscher, W. C.; **Keys to Woody Plants**, Comstock Publishing Associates, Ithaca, New York, 1955.

New England Section, Society of American Foresters; **Important Tree Pests of the Northeast**, Evans Printing Company, Concord, New Hampshire, 1952.

Panshin, A. J. and de Zeeuw, Carl; **Textbook of Wood Technology**, McGraw-Hill Book Company, Toronto; 4th Ed., 1980.

Roland, A. E. and Smith, E. C.; **The Flora of Nova Scotia**, N.S. Institute of Science, Halifax, 1969.

Scoggan, H. J.; **The Flora of Canada**, National Museum of Natural Sciences Pub. No. 7 (1-4), Ottawa, 1978.

U. S. Department of Agriculture; **Trees: The Yearbook of Agriculture, 1949**.

———; **Silvics of Forest Trees of the United States** (Agricultural Bull. No. 271), 1965.

Zim, H. S. and Martin, A. C.; **Trees: A Guide to Familiar American Trees**, Golden Press, New York, 1963.

INDEX